# Emotional Manipulation: An Assault on Our Democracy

Philippe Jaquenod

A catalogue record for this
book is available from the
National Library of Australia

Copyright © 2025 Philippe Jaquenod
ISBN-13: 978-1-923174-48-1

Linellen Press
265 Boomerang Road
Oldbury, Western Australia
www.linellenpress.com.au

*Democracy is a process, not a static condition. It is becoming, rather than being. It can be easily lost but is never finally won.*

(William H. Hastie)

*A society that puts equality...ahead of freedom will end up with neither equality nor freedom...a society that puts freedom first will, as a happy by-product, end up with both greater freedom and greater equality.*

(Milton Freedman)

**The Cover**

The artwork in the front and back covers are an artist's representation of the theme of the book. Woke elites have managed to climb to the top of the tree of democracy and have thrown ordinary Australians into a new cultural prison from which they desperately wish to escape.

# About this Book

We are living in a period of history where emotions are clouding our better judgment.

Our culture is dominated by ideology and we are witnessing the demise of sound, independent intellectual thought. Our Australian universities have become the bastion of the rising woke ideology, and our freedom of expression and belief is facing threats previously unknown to post-World War 2 generations.

In this book, Philippe Jaquenod identifies a new set of ten 21st century "virtues", crafted by the new woke "elites". These virtues have perniciously permeated all levels of administration and government, and they provide the bad "oxygen" required to sustain the emotional crisis our nation is experiencing.

Such is the onslaught on our hearts and minds that many hardworking Australians have become discouraged and disengaged. As a result, we are now witnessing the rise of a new type of *forgotten people*, (some might even say *abandoned*) whose political weariness offers little resistance to the relentless onslaught to which they are being subjected.

Some hard questions need to be raised: what can we do to stop our Australian democracy from backsliding? Or are we already so brainwashed that we do not even realise that we are innocent pawns in a new game of emotional manipulation?

There is still time to resist, and this book offers some solutions, but more importantly, the author hopes that many will enlist to fight a new type of enemy formerly not encountered on our Australian shores.

Written in an easy English language style, this book is essential reading for all informed and thinking Australians; for all who care about the future of their children and grandchildren in this great country of ours.

# About the Author

**Philippe Jaquenod**, a father of three adult children, made Australia home more than fifty years ago when he arrived in Sydney as a young adult. Philippe has a rich background in social activism, business, finance and political research. He holds a Bachelor of Arts from Macquarie University and is an Australian-qualified translator in the French and English languages.

Philippe is also the author of *Silent, Fragile and Isolated*, published by Linellen Press in 2022.

# Dedication and Acknowledgements

This book is first dedicated to the memory of my father, Pierre, and my mother, Georgette, who, under very challenging circumstances, made financial and emotional sacrifices well beyond the call of duty for my Christian upbringing and my education.

I also dedicate this book to the thousands of Australians who make up a new generation of "forgotten people", to those whose opinions are not heard or listened to, and to those who have nobody to represent them properly in the corridors of power.

My acknowledgements also go to those who have participated in the production of this book, and in particular, to my wife M for her suggestions, patient proofreading and editing and to my very capable friend H.D. for offering highly valuable additional content, constructive criticism and grammatical corrections.

Nevertheless, the ultimate responsibility for the final product is exclusively and naturally mine.

# Contents

# Introduction

## The questions that matter

*"The art and science of asking questions is the source
of all knowledge".*

(Thomas Berger)

In my former book, *Silent, Fragile and Isolated, (Linelien Press 2022),* I explained how our intellectual capital is in the process of being slowly eroded and replaced with an appeal to a certain set of unjustifiable emotions, which has contributed to the fragilisation and the isolation of each and every member of our Australian society.

I focused then on the loss of our freedom of speech and religious liberty and deplored the isolation into which we now find ourselves, condemned to silence for fear of reprisal by a woke movement not interested in debate.

This work now takes the argument further and explores how the ruling classes (particularly those left-of-centre) are appealing to a certain type of emotions, channelled through a number of centres of influence, in order to control the behaviour of the general population and, most importantly, how votes are cast at the ballot box.

It is a form of neo-colonialism, and democracy is endangered whilst approval to govern is obtained through psychological manipulation, maybe even by way of false pretences.

A surprising set of ten new moral/emotional values are instrumental to this form of new dominance. They are:

- Outrage
- Fear
- Guilt
- Authenticity
- Empathy
- Humility
- Self-care
- Vulnerability
- Envy, and
- Love.

They will be the focus of our discussion in Chapter Four. I am saying "new" because, until now, most of these have never been elevated to the status of "virtue", and others, such as humility, empathy and love, have been comprehensively redefined and bear no resemblance to the definitions that, until recently, stood the test of time.

These so-called new virtues are the product of the hypocritical and largely self-appointed "elites" or chattering classes/elected representatives who are not really interested in changing the circumstances of their less fortunate human beings but who are rather focused on virtue signalling to promote their own particular ideological brand.

Their position in society, whether elected representatives, media people, academics, art world celebrities or the like, assures them access to a ready-made public podium, out of reach for most of us mere "plebeians". As such, their message is broadcast through megaphones that simply drown out the weaker voices of the average Australian. Their astonishing ability to 'stay on message' and, the sheer repetition of their ill-founded assertions, their insistence on seeing everything through the narrow prism of their worldview eventually give them the victory they have been looking for: the indoctrination of the people.

But worst still, this regrettable outcome is further reinforced by a substantial degree of indifference to all things political on the part of the average Australian or at least by a feeling of powerlessness anchored in distrust towards politicians and established institutions.

Some questions need to be raised: what happens at the ballot box? Is a significant proportion of the total votes merely the outcome of emotional indoctrination? Are Australians manipulated into feeling guilty in voting any other way than the "elites" want them to? Are Australians even aware of the impact of emotional political manipulation?

Emotions, indeed, seem to prevail everywhere. Serious thinking, on the other hand, is in decline.

None of this, of course, has occurred overnight. Rather it is the outcome of a gradual slide, a slippery slope on which we embarked long ago. I discussed some of this in *Silent, Fragile and Isolated*, arguing that the starting point is as distant to our present times now as the 17th century Enlightenment and I do not propose to revisit this historical analysis here.

Rather, my focus will be on the sociological model of the West, that is to say, capitalism and free enterprise, on which the Australian governance system has relied to date.

Although far better than socialism and its rebellious offspring – communism – capitalism is now starting to show a number of cracks that we should not ignore.

Unfortunately, it appears that these cracks are not in the process of being plastered, and consequently, a void is emerging that emotional manipulation is attempting to fill.

Having brushed away recourse to the solace of religion, the West thought it could build a solid foundation on the plank of capitalism, promising riches, happiness, and contentment for all, and whilst Bob Hawke's foolish promise[1] will always remain a chimera, a nice utopian dream in itself, capitalism has certainly made a big dent in world poverty.

For instance, the real Gross Domestic Product (GDP) of the United States, Australia, Germany, Canada, Japan, France and the United Kingdom has soared over the last two hundred years and life expectancy at birth has increased for everyone.[2]

On the other hand, among nations where capitalism has been and continues to be rejected, the alternative model, socialism, or worse still, its communist offspring, has resulted in wars, genocide, injustice and poverty.

Socialism and communism correctly identified that capitalism presented some dangers. The socialists imagined that capitalism might prove to be a dangerous tool, once placed into the hands of greedy, self-centred individuals. Unfortunately, the remedy they offered soon proved to be worse than the so-called disease.

For a while, it was thought that capitalism and socialism would balance each other and lead the world towards a new "equilibrium" (to use an economic term) where peace, riches and justice would prevail.

For a while, indeed, it was thought that socialism and capitalism would blend in, converge towards each other and produce a new haven of peace and prosperity.

These were the days when convergence theory was very much in vogue.

---

[1] Bob Hawke famously claimed on 23rd June 1987 that by 1990 no child would live in poverty in Australia

[2] https://humanprogress.org/trends/ (accessed 20/11/2023)

The 1960s brainchild of US professor Clark Kerr, convergence theory postulated indeed that weaker economies would eventually catch up to or converge towards stronger economies due to the law of diminishing returns, whereby at a particular point in time, past optimum, each additional unit of input yields a smaller increase of output.

This meant that at some stage, well-established economies would produce lesser returns whilst, in contrast, developing nations would display greater ones, thus starting to catch up with the rest of the world.

To some extent, this is still true in the sense that a fairly large number of lesser-developed countries are currently enjoying greater rates of growth in their Gross National Product than their more economically established Western counterparts. For instance, recent rates of annual growth achieved as of July 2023 for countries around the world comprise Senegal 8.3%, Fiji 7%, Ethiopia 6.1%, Vietnam 5.1% and Uganda 5.7%, in sharp contrast with the United States 1.8%, Australia 1.6%, France 1.8% and Germany -0.3%.[3]

Yet, these comparisons are simplistic. It is naïve to attempt to describe capitalism just by reference to rates of growth of the national product.

This is so because, beyond GDP, capitalism has unique features that are diametrically opposed to those of the socialist States.

In a recent publication[4], retired academic Christo Moskovsky paints a striking but realistically accurate contrast between the two types of society.

---

[3] Wikipedia, list of countries by real GDP growth rates (list 2023 July) https://en.wikipedia.org/wiki/List_of_countries_by_real_GDP_growth_rate sourced 17/08/2023
[4] "It keeps pointing left", Christo Moskovsky, IPA Review, Volume 75/2, p.52-54. Institute of Public Affairs Ltd, Melbourne.

He sees Western capitalism featuring political pluralism, a politically unaligned security apparatus, a free and independent media, a community of autonomous individuals, a vibrant and mostly privately owned industry sector, some level of unemployment and last but not least, a sense of dignity of work.

On the other hand, his view of socialism features a one-party system, a complete fusion between the State and the security services, a State-controlled media, a community essentially consisting of two castes – the ruling class (or Nomenklatura) and the commoners (plebs) who essentially have no rights, a State-controlled industry, a centrally planned economy, full employment at all times and a feeling that work is a drag.

Now, this is where convergence theory fails: sociologically, these two diametrically opposed systems do not converge towards each other.

A communist country such as China, for instance, might happily accept some technology, some degree of innovation and even joint ventures with Western world interests, but this is always on the State's terms, ensuring that the State keeps the upper hand, the ultimate control over any investment and over the lives of its people.

Yes, socialist regimes still remain fundamentally fiercely socialist.

Unfortunately, the West is failing due to the growing influence of the socialist "elites" who occupy the major cities of the capitalist world.

Indeed, the Western world seems now to be moving inexorably towards the East, allowing governments to take an increasing role in our private lives, interfering with liberties and freedom of expression in ways that would have been unimaginable a century ago.

There is, therefore, convergence but only from one side. It is not the poorer becoming richer but rather all but the very wealthy becoming poorer, both economically and qualitatively.

Millions of people all around the globe, who live under a capitalist system feel discouraged, powerless and alienated.

A new class is emerging in capitalist Western-style societies and in Australia. This is the class of the forgotten ones.

Not forgotten in the Menzian political sense but forgotten in a new sense which we have not experienced before.

Menzies' reference to the forgotten ones in his eloquent 1942 speech was focused on the middle class; they were not economically at the bottom of the ladder but neither were they near the top. They were not rich but they were 'the battlers', to use a term coined by John Howard some thirty years ago now.

Yes, nowadays, the forgotten ones are not Menzies' middle classes of shopkeepers and self-employed tradesmen, neither are they the economic battlers of John Howard.

No, the forgotten ones, nowadays, are a mass of apolitical, disillusioned, frustrated, alienated people who feel disempowered and who are engaged in manual and non-manual trades and occupations. They have little faith in our institutions, our parliaments, our courts and even our police. They battle against bureaucracy, high interest rates and significant levels of debt.

We could label them "the unrepresented" or the new "Misérables" of our times, but these vignettes do not describe the fundamental issue at stake: they are the overlooked people, ignored, passed over by our various levels of government and institutions. Their fundamental gripe is not necessarily economic but more simply this: they are unhappy, and their voices are ignored. We could even say that they have been somewhat abandoned.

I am not talking about Aboriginal populations living in squalor in remote areas, out of sight and out of mind. They are part of the forgotten ones in the sense that billions of dollars of taxpayers' money, destined to improve their dismal state of affairs, never really reach them. A large proportion of the funds allocated to them are appropriated 'en route' by a disinterested bureaucracy and by agencies established with the purported sole purpose of caring for them.

Indeed, these isolated communities form part of the cohort of forgotten ones, but they are only a minute fraction of it.

The majority of the people I am referring to makes up a very large proportion of the Australian population. They mostly live in our larger cities. They are Europeans, Asians, Australian-born or overseas-born, religious as well as atheists. We find them among different generations although they appear to be overrepresented among the young.

Let me be more precise.

According to the Australian Bureau of Statistics, 46% of young women and 31% of young men aged 16-24 are currently experiencing a mental disorder. In total, 39% of young people are suffering from a mental disorder, compared to 27% in 1997.[5]

Furthermore, the 2023 Edelman survey[6] revealed that less than 50% of voters now trust government; also, economic optimism has collapsed, and nuclear war, climate change, energy shortages and food shortages are becoming topics of increasing concern among Australians.

A recent State of the Nation Survey revealed that 68% of a random sample of 13,000 Australians were dissatisfied with the way the nation is headed.[7]

---

[5] Cited in Watercooler News, Watercooler#293 Why are young people so depressed, Centre for Youth Policy, Menzies Research Centre.
[6] https://www.edelman.com/trust/2023/trust-barometer
[7] https://www.news.com.au/national/federal-election/state-of-the-nation-survey-reveals-68-per-cent-of-aussies-unhappy-with-the-direction-country-is-heading-in/news-story/7500cf52287c9b8d869e92b78a3aabe4 (sourced 29/08/2023)

The media also reported that *"Australian workers are in poorer physical and mental health since the pandemic across all ages and stages; prime-aged workers – those between 25 and 55 – are reporting the greatest burn-out. Some 50% of prime-aged workers…feel exhausted at work. About 40% reported feeling less motivated about their work than pre-pandemic, and 33% found it more difficult to concentrate at work because of responsibilities outside of work".*[8]

According to the 2022 Australian Election Study, *"54% of voters believe that government is run for a few big interests while 12% believe that government is run for all people".*[9]

The evidence is indeed overwhelming, and this alarming state of affairs is now impacting political involvement at the grassroots level. People do not see the point of voting anymore. They do it more out of compulsion than out of a conviction that this might help them in their personal circumstances, or even benefit the country as a whole.

Indeed, according to the Australia Institute, voter turnout at the 2022 Federal election hit a new low.[10] For the first time since compulsory voting was introduced in 1925, voter turnout dropped below 90%. Also, the informal vote, which hovered around 3% in the 1990s, is now over 5%.[11]

This problem is not unique to Australia. A recent OECD report on the Drivers of Trust in Public Institutions has revealed

[8] https://theconversation.com/the-great-resignation-didnt-happen-in-australia-but-the-great-burnout-did-201173 (sourced 29/08/2023)

[9] https://australianelectionstudy.org/wp-content/uploads/The-2022-Australian-Federal-Election-Results-from-the-Australian-Election-Study.pdf, p.25 (accessed 02/11/2023)

[10] https://australiainstitute.org.au/post/voter-turnout-in-the-2022-federal-election-hit-a-new-low-threatening-our-democratic-tradition/ (sourced 29/08/2023)

[11] https://www.aec.gov.au/voting/informal_voting/summary.htm (sourced 29/08/2023)

that 44 per cent of respondents across 30 member countries have low or no trust in their national government.[12]

Why do Australians feel so disempowered? Why have they lost trust not only in government, but in authority and in the broader institutions that have been such an important part of our Australian society: legislative, judiciary and executive?

How do governments deal with them? How is it that such a large proportion of Australians are part of the "forgotten ones"? How is it that governments get re-elected over and over again by voters who do not like them? How do governments manage to get their support at the ballot box? If these voters are emotionally manipulated, then how?

Does the disengagement of these people threaten the very fabric of our society? Our freedom of expression? Our religious beliefs? Or the role of the church? Are we now already both post-religious and post-democratic?

These are some of the important questions that all thinking Australians should ask themselves, questions that this book will endeavour to address.

They are, indeed, the questions that matter.

---

[12] As reported in the Week End Australian, July 20-21 2024, *Rising anxiety as trust takes a tumble.* p.20

# Chapter 1

## A tale of two classes (and more than two cities)

*"A multitude of people and yet a solitude."*

(Charles Dickens)

What is a noble lie?

The concept of the noble lie was introduced by the ancient Greek philosopher Plato.

In his book, *The Republic,* Plato makes a distinction between three classes of people. The golden class is made up of the governing bodies, silver is the army or auxiliary services and bronze is the working population. This is the parable of the metals.

In today's parlance, we could say that these are the equivalents of our parliamentarians (gold class), our public service (silver class) and the rest of us (bronze class).

According to Plato, the golden class (the elites) feeds a lie to the working population relying on the assistance of the silver class auxiliary services in order to preserve the existing social harmony among the "bronze" people. In other words, the elites, with the auxiliary support of the nation's institutions (schools, universities, courts, police and armed forces), deliver a message that is not true, but the contents of this message shall, nevertheless, hopefully, appease the masses for their own good.

Dear reader, you might have guessed it: as Plato, I, too, believe that we have been fed a number of noble lies in Australia.

Unfortunately, none of these are for our own good although the elites would seem to believe they are.

We are manipulated into believing these lies through appeal to our emotions.

What are these noble lies might you say?

There is, of course, the lie of the environmental movement, the lie of the diversity movement, the lie that activism trumps education, the lie that all Jews are bad, the lie that all Palestinians are good, the lie that all white males are bad, the lie that all black men are good, the lie that all religions are the enemies of peace and also, of course, the lie that the welfare state will comprehensively take care of all your needs and, dear reader, you will probably think of a few more of these lies as well!

The list seems, indeed, to be endless.

Lies usually have consequences. However, unlike Plato's noble lie, the lies of our 21st-century Australia are not bringing a form of submission, of peace, or even of faked shalom, so to speak. These lies, unfortunately, bring down division and conflict and lead to a segregated, isolated society.

This sociological isolation has made many of us feel that we are forgotten citizens – overlooked, ignored by those in office, by the very ones who are meant to represent us in the corridors of power.

So prevalent is this feeling of isolation that even those who are not genuinely forgotten appear to believe they are: they feel the welfare state, for all its subsidies, grants, pensions and other significant largesse, is, in fact, letting them down.

The genuinely forgotten and the claiming-to-be-forgotten: the statistics cited earlier cover both categories and eventually, each becomes a challenge for any government. Yet, their mindsets and aspirations are polar opposites.

Furthermore, whilst both categories remain the victims of political emotional manipulation, the means exercised by the left-of-centre political parties to control them vary significantly.

Who are these people?

The genuinely forgotten are usually found among the self-reliant, hard-working classes who do not enjoy the privilege of family wealth and high society connections.

They are those Max Weber[13] would have described as portraying "the Protestant ethic". They believe in the ethical dimension of hard work, the duty one has to contribute one's talents to society; they are also those who hold on to the expectation of being treated and rewarded justly.

Many of them who demonstrate this work ethic are genuinely forgotten because our political, educational and legislative bodies no longer represent them. The genuinely forgotten are forgotten because their ideology no longer accords itself with that of our institutions and elected representatives.

In particular, they do not fit into the new, or relatively new, Australian welfare state.

To resort to a well-known biblical expression, they are "sojourners in a foreign land".

The aspirations they have for themselves and their children are frustrated by an elite ideology they cannot accept.

This category of Australians includes religious and non-religious people who believe in freedom of speech, birth-defined gender and self-reliance. They tend to be proud to be Australians and, in the main, feel positive about the place Australia holds in the world as well as about its past achievements. They believe in giving a "hand up" but generally oppose government "handouts".

---

[13] Weber Max, The Protestant ethic and the Spirit of Capitalism, Oxford University Press, rev.1920 ed.

On the other hand, the claiming-to-be-forgotten believe in a universal minimum wage, curtailment of free speech, the closure of private schools, the suppression of religious belief and punitive rates of taxation on the rich; in other words, their view of government is big brother government.

They feel that they are forgotten but this is only because they have placed an over-reliance on the role of government in their lives. They want more and more and are prepared to give less and less.

In my country of birth, they are represented by the Yellow-vests people and those who burn cars, erect street barricades, and throw Molotov cocktails because their government wants them to work a couple more years before they can retire.

In other words, these are persons who are not all necessarily economically poor but who feel insecure and who consider themselves to be the victims of an unjust society.

The higher their perceived insecurity (subjective or not), the higher their perception of being disadvantaged is, which in turn leads us to conclude that no amount of monetary assistance is going to make them feel that they are being treated fairly.

Their sphere of influence is deplorably far too significant. Their key emotion is anger. Their weapon of choice is mass protest. Their key recriminations revolve around the ecological future of the planet, the cost of living and their unique view of social justice.

I argue that they are not a class of genuinely forgotten citizens because they already attract an excessive amount of attention among the media, the "elites" and the educational institutions. Their level of parliamentary representation in Australia is on the rise; they gain their support from the Teal "independents", the unions, the more left-leaning factions of the Labor Party and the Greens.

What of those I consider to be genuinely forgotten?

Their source of discontent lies elsewhere. They are concerned about the rise of the bureaucracy, government intrusion into the private sphere, the loss of parental rights, the threat to freedom of speech, educational brainwashing, multiculturalism and attacks on the rule of law. The level of parliamentary representation of the genuinely forgotten people is low or at least on the decline. Their support in the past revolved around the centre of politics and a generally held consensus supporting the value of free enterprise, risk and reward, family and nation.

The genuinely forgotten are unhappy but they are not particularly vocal. With some few but notable exceptions, they are not the ones who walk the streets with banners or arrange rallies in front of Parliament House. It is too easy to label them "conservative" because that epithet conveys a sense of opposition to change and yet, they are not anti-change: they merely do not want change that destroys their fundamental freedoms, their right to worship, their right to bring their children up within the framework of their values, their right to be rewarded for effort and responsible risk-taking. They do not often write to or call on their local Member of Parliament. They feel that doing so would be a waste of time. They expect they will only get a standard reply written by some underling, with no offer of a tangible solution, no sympathy, let alone empathy for their case.

These forgotten ones are prone to be conformists. Unfortunately, conformity paves the way for the demise of democracy.

As Aldous Huxley wrote in his *Brave New World*:

> *A really efficient totalitarian state would be one in which the all-powerful executive of political bosses and their army of managers control a population of*

*slaves who do not have to be coerced, because they love their servitude.*[14]

It seems that a significant amount of the Australian population does not like to "make any fuss". This is not just politically, but in every day's situations as well. These are the people who are served a very badly cooked dish at a restaurant but who will not return it and prefer to eat it and pay for it rather than being seen to be "difficult".

More significantly, both the genuinely forgotten and the claim-to-be-forgotten are frustrated by three major influential sets of circumstances beyond their control: globalism, post-nationalism and economic mismanagement.

They are the cracks of our capitalist system.

It is to these that we now need to turn our attention.

---

[14] Quoted in *Our Culture of Conformity Makes it Difficult to Defeat the Voice, Gabriel A. Moens, Spectator Australia, 9 October 2023.*

# Chapter 2

## The Seismic Cracks in Australian Society

*"The most tragic paradox of our time is to be found in the failure of nation-states to recognise the imperatives of internationalism."*

(Earl Warren)

What are the cracks that seem to be appearing in our Australian democratic liberal system?

Are these serious?

Are these getting larger?

Is there a risk that the whole edifice of our society could suddenly crash down with a loud and fearful-sounding thump?

What is really wrong with free enterprise? Has it not served our country really well?

There is no doubt that a cursory glance at our situation will reveal that Australia has been the "lucky country". Overall, our economic system has delivered significant benefits to most households in Australia.

In a recent report, the Australian Productivity Commission attests to these facts.

*"What distinguishes Australia from most other developed countries has been its unprecedented 27-year period of uninterrupted economic growth, prompting many to ask how the economic gains from*

17

*growth have been shared. While growth is no guarantee against a widening disparity between rich and poor, we show that it has delivered for the average Australian household in every income decile significantly improved living standards. This is in contrast with the United States (which had a similar rate of increase in income inequality as Australia) where the distribution is much more uneven, with income growth in the lower deciles about a quarter of that for Australian households".[15]*

A great score card, indeed, for Australia.

So, what is the problem?

There are a number of factors at play which we will consider in turn: globalisation, deglobalisation, post-nationalism, economic mismanagement, poor ethics and corruption, the impact of artificial intelligence on human rights, the hypocrisy of the "elites" and the demise of the justice system. Taken separately, they do not threaten capitalism as an economic system, yet they undermine the fundamental planks on which capitalism stands: the right to hold to one's own thoughts, the right to free speech, the reward for individual effort and for delayed gratification and the rule of law.

In other words: liberal democracy.

## Globalisation

Whilst this is not a book about economics, it needs to be said at the outset that, by and large, Western world governments (capitalist nations, if you prefer) have now lost a degree of control over the countries they represent.

---

[15] Rising Inequality, a Stocktake of the Evidence, Productivity Research Paper, August 2018, Productivity Commission Research Paper, Canberra

Globalisation affects us all.

Australia is no exception.

Globalisation has impacted us for some time and a number of academics have already sounded the alarm.

For instance, in their book *Rethinking Capitalism*[16], Malcolm Jacobs and Mariana Mazzucato point out that capitalism is no longer producing stable growth. They argue that the total share of labour and wages has fallen and that the distribution of the reduced labour share has become more unequal, with a greater proportion going to those at the top of the earnings scale.

Taking this argument further, Emeritus Professor Colin Crouch argues that much of the economic instability witnessed in recent years has been the result of the rise of the "giant firm" and that "transnational corporations have outgrown the capacity of individual nation-states".[17]

In *The Crisis of Democratic Capitalism*, Martin Wolf, Chief Economics Commentator at the Financial Times, also writes:

> *"The health of our societies depends on sustaining a delicate balance between the economic and the political, the individual and the collective, the national and the global. But that balance is broken. Our economy has destabilised our politics and vice versa. **We are no longer able to combine the operations of the market economy with stable liberal democracy.** (my emphasis). A big part of the reason for this is that the economy is not delivering the security and widely shared prosperity expected by large parts of our societies".[18]*

---

[16]Jacobs & Mazzucato, Rethinking Capitalism, Economics Policy for Sustainable Growth, John Wiley & Sons 2016

[17] Colin Crouch, Post Democracy After the Crise, Polity Press, 2020

[18] Martin Wolf, The Crisis of Democratic Capitalism, Penguin, 2023, p.11

We are indeed living in insecure times, and the days have gone by where people stayed in a particular occupation for most of their working lives.

According to the Australian Bureau of Statistics there were 13.8 million people employed in February 2023. A staggering 56% had been employed in their current job for less than 5 years; 21% had been in their job for less than 1 year and only about 10% had been in their current job for 20 years or more.[19]

Insecurity is an issue, but it is only one. Others, such as Princeton University's Anne Case and Angus Deaton, consider the problem to be more of an issue of unfairness.[20]

They write from an American perspective but much of what they observe applies also to Australia. They see that a major cause of unfairness is the practice of rent-seeking: the generation of income obtained by the manipulation of social or political factors without creating new wealth.

Is this economic rent-seeking a form of manipulation of the market, in other words, some sort of "fightback" against economic deregulation?

Is it a realisation by governments that globalisation might have taken us too far, in some respects at least? It might be, but unfortunately, it allows ideology to set in. It allows governments to select winners by allocating subsidies to causes that support the new "morality", the new "diversity", an issue we will discuss at some length further on.

---

[19] https://www.abs.gov.au/statistics/labour/jobs/job-mobility/feb-2023#key-statistics (sourced 07/09/2023)
[20] Anne Case & Angus Deaton, Deaths of Despair and the Future of Capitalism, Princeton University, 2020

## Post-nationalism

Whilst the 20th-century phenomenon of the globalisation of our economy has attracted much commentary in the past, it would seem that the concept of post-nationalism is not forefront of the public mind. This is unfortunate, for it is a development that is gradually having a major impact on our lives.

In many countries, post-nationalism is the logical progression of a philosophy of failed multiculturalism.

This happens to be also the case for Australia.

Properly understood, multiculturalism is the acceptance of foreign cultures into the host nation in a way that allows them to maintain their own traditions and beliefs without harming the host nation's fundamental values and way of life.

However, multiculturalism in Australia has proven to be a different phenomenon.

In the latter part of the twentieth century, immigration was still fitting the above definition: migrants, such as I, brought their own culture to this land but in a manner that only enriched the Australian culture because it was not inimical to the fundamental Judeo-Christian values on which our country had been established. For instance, new foods, new types of entertainment and new sports were introduced, adding to but in no way subtracting from those already in vogue in Australia.

In more recent years, however, the Australian brand of multiculturalism has, unfortunately, metamorphosed into something quite different, resembling more closely the definition provided by Encyclopedia Britannica:

> *"Multiculturalism is the view that cultures, races and ethnicities, particularly those of **minority groups**, deserve **special acknowledgement** (my emphasis) of their differences within a dominant political culture".*

*Indeed, it is by espousing this particular definition of multiculturalism that our country has fallen into the trap of fostering the very group identities and group values that define the woke movement.*

From thereon, it has not been difficult to allow philosophies originating from outside our shores to influence and fashion a new way of thinking.

This is what post-nationalism is all about. It is a phenomenon that originates from outside the nation, outside its borders, it is beyond our shores, and it comes in, often uninvited, and it starts remodelling the values of our nation.

Post-nationalism is highly multi-faceted. For instance, it has a strong economic dimension, and an obvious example of economic post-nationalism is the case of the European Union. Members of the Union are constrained by the economic policies dictated by the Union. Yes, each country has representation in the European Parliament, but in the final analysis, each needs to bow to what the majority decides in terms of national budget restrictions, overseas trade and the like.

Nevertheless, post-nationalism is, first and foremost, a sociological phenomenon for the simple reason that national economies are the reflection of the key priorities endorsed by their respective societies.

This is not a new issue: already in 1998, the German philosopher Jurgen Habermas discussed post-nationalism in his *Die Postnationale Konstellation,* later translated into English under the title *The Postnational Constellation.* In that book, Habermas acknowledged that globalisation was not going to disappear and that Europe was likely to become a constellation of post-national states, as evidenced by the formation of the EU, established five years prior to the publication of his work in 1993.

All of this very much applies to Australia. Our country is no longer a distant colonial bastion of Mother England. It boasts a highly cosmopolitan population and is influenced in its economic and cultural makeup by Asia, Europe and the United States. Above all, however, it is influenced by a new way of thinking that continues to put pressure on our institutions but which does not originate from within our borders and is instead propelled by social media and the Internet.

In this regard, it would also be foolish to ignore the influence that the United Nations is exerting upon Australia.

Take, for instance, the UN International Covenant on the Rights of Indigenous Peoples (UNICRIP) to which Australia has been a signatory since the days of Gough Whitlam. This is a document embedded in extreme ideology. Space does not allow me to go through each of its articles, but reference to article 5 should suffice to make the point: Article 5 of UNICRIP specifically states that Indigenous peoples have the right to self-determination and to run their "distinct, political, legal, economic, social and cultural institutions… whilst retaining their right, if they so choose, to participate fully in the political, economic, social and cultural life of the State". [21]

In other words, create a separatist autonomous political state within the nation of Australia.

Alarmingly, this type of new influence is understandably fostering a number of tensions among a large segment of the Australian population, which includes those I have labelled earlier as *forgotten ones* and which, in some instances, such as in the case of the Jewish Australians, should be referred to as the *abandoned ones*.

---

[21] https://www.un.org/development/desa/indigenouspeoples/wp-content/uploads/sites/19/2018/11/UNDRIP_E_web.pdf (accessed 13/10/2024)

The question of what binds us together as a nation is, indeed, becoming increasingly difficult to answer. The failed *Voice* referendum makes the point. Although the referendum failed, the very idea of presenting it to the Australian people confirms that we are no longer united: discrimination on the grounds of race is well entrenched.

For instance, whilst Australia has not yet (mercifully) incorporated the full text of the UNICRIP into our domestic law, it is clear that this type of United Nations agreement is influencing many of our local institutions. As leading Australian investigative journalist, Janet Albrechtsen recently wrote: *"the separatist spirit of the Voice lives on in thousands of corporate action programs'*[22] and many of our leading corporate institutions, such as BHP and Coles, have adopted a Reconciliation Action Plan approved by Reconciliation Australia, a body funded by the Federal Government, which in turn promotes the extreme ideology of the UNICRIP Convention.

Australia is also undoubtedly influenced by China.

Indeed, in their recently published book, *The Unlucky Country,* accomplished Australian academics Augusto Zimmerman and Gabriel Moens remind us that:

> *"Beijing launders donations through a network of Confucius Institutes to about a dozen Australian universities…These Chinese studies institutes may teach language, but they have become centres for Chinese government intelligence and control, including monitoring and censorship of those who stray off the academic paths with which Beijing is comfortable. The situation becomes even more bizarre when we know that a considerable number of*

---

[22] Janet Albrechtsen, The secret agenda CEOs may have missed in Indigenous plans", The Week-End Australian 12-13 October 2024, p.18

*Australian universities accommodate centres for Islamic studies and that, directly or indirectly, these centres receive money donated by countries such as United Arab Emirates, Qatar, Turkey, and Iran directly or indirectly. As for the sort of "academic work" provided by such centres, in 2013, the ANU Centre for Islamic Studies hosted a speaker, Richard Falk, who dismissed concerns about Ayatollah Khomeini's summary executions, repression of women and human rights abuses as "happily false".*[23]

What are the consequences then of these post nationalist trends in Australia?

Clearly, they are instability, division, anxiety and insecurity.

Indeed, the Australian people are increasingly feeling insecure and threatened by both elected representatives who are not interested in listening and by international bodies and institutions that hold and wish to impose diametrically opposed values to their own.

Most of us would have some familiarity with the concept of "world government". Many of us still dismiss the concept as being over alarmingly conspiratory, and whilst this writer does not subscribe to the view that a single mortal human being will ever preside over the government of the entire world, I am still of the view that we are already witnessing the dawn of world government, compliments of post-nationalism.

The expansion of post-nationalism is largely fuelled by the propagation of the new woke moral order and its distinctive values. Once this philosophy becomes the new gospel of at least a majority of the so-called leading nations of the world, once the

---

[23] Zimmerman A & Moens G, The Unlucky Country, Locke Press 2024, p.30 (PDF version)

separate and individual decisions of most governments on this planet are aligned with the values of a new woke morality, we can imagine that most outcomes will be the same as if a single invisible hand were guiding the decisions and behaviours of the peoples of the world. One world with one mindset would then be the mark of what we understand by world government. No democracy as we understand it, but a totalitarian regime where people might still foolishly believe they have a say in the affairs of their country, unaware that they have become the very puppets of a new world order.

And whilst this is unfolding progressively, the very essence of our Australian democracy continues to be under attack.

How? What examples can we point to support this contention?

Too many, alas, but to mention just a few, may I ask, for instance, how many of the Australian forgotten people would agree with the support given by the Australian Centre for International Justice to have international arrest warrants issued against Israel's Benjamin Netanyahu for his role in the Gaza conflict?[24]

Or would many Australians agree about granting significant powers to the World Health Organisation that might result in drastic measures being automatically implemented in the case of a new health emergency in our country? Yet, this is what is currently being proposed.[25]

Indeed, if democracy is the result of separate individual decisions taken without duress or undue influence by the majority of our Australian voters, can we then have true

---

[24] https://acij.org.au/media-release-australia-must-support-landmark-icc-application-for-arrest-warrants-in-the-situation-in-palestine/ accessed 17/07/2024

[25] Balancing public health and human rights, The Spectator Magazine, 8 June 2023

democracy once our emotions and intellects have been polluted by the values of a majority of other nations with different mindsets, traditions and cultural norms?

Can you have democracy without a specific national culture, specific national values peculiar to a particular country? Can Australia be democratic if it ceases to be Australian? Can France be democratic if it ceases to be French? Can England be democratic if it ceases to be English? This writer does not think so.

The experience of the European Union seems to give weight to this argument.

In Europe, it would seem that a common multinational democracy is the EU's idea of utopia.

In Europe, national cultures differ from each other. The North and the South think differently and feel differently. In a country such as Sweden, the State has a more intrusive role than in France, the Germans have a different mindset than the Italians and the English have a Westminster system of government unique in Europe.

Brexit was the result of a clash of cultures between a Brussels mindset and a British mindset. The former wanted to reach out into all spheres: the family, the environment, the law, and the economy, whilst the latter resented this involvement as intrusion or, dare I say it, as an assault on the values that define the United Kingdom and its right to self-government.

In a document entitled *The Benefits of Brexit; how the UK is taking advantage of leaving the EU*[26], the UK government writes that *"the objective of leaving the EU has been to restore the UK as a sovereign independent country so that we can once again determine our*

---

26

https://assets.publishing.service.gov.uk/media/620a791d8fa8f54915f4369e/benefits-of-brexit.pdf (accessed 10/11/2023) *own future".*

It seems that the UK has realised that European culture is becoming increasingly alien to British culture. The influence of Brussels on social and economic policy is one factor but the issue of migration is probably the key factor.

In his bestseller *The Strange Death of Europe,* Douglas Murray made a similar point a few years ago:

*"By the middle of this century, while China will probably still look like China, India will still probably look like India, Russia like Russia and Eastern Europe like Eastern Europe, Western Europe will at best resemble a large-scale version of the United Nations…but it will not be Europe anymore".[27]*

We are deluding ourselves into thinking that Australia is a different case because of our relative geographical isolation. Immigration is changing our culture, and our left-of-centre governments are increasingly successful at manipulating the Australian electorate into feeling guilty for opposing large scale immigration, particularly, of course, refugees. And whilst on humanitarian grounds, few would demand a complete cessation of all genuine refugee migrants, the influx of migrants from other cultures is one of the main ways in which our culture of democratic liberalism is threatened.

Some might retort that such a claim is a bit "rich" coming from a writer who is not Australian-born. However, when I came here in the 1970s, I made the decision to accept the Australian culture, its values and its system of government. I had no agenda and still believe that this was the best decision of my life. I wrote this book, and I wrote *Silent, Fragile and Isolated,* because I love Australia, and I do not want to see it going the way Europe has.

---

[27] Douglas Murray, The Strange Death of Europe, Immigration, Identity Islam, Bloomsbury Publishing, 2017, p.309-310.

Globalisation, post-nationalism, and immigration are threatening the fabric of our Australian culture. These events have brought about tension, anxiety and discord among a growing number of the "forgotten ones". In a later chapter, we shall explore how our Australian governments "manage" this state of affairs through political emotional manipulation.

At this stage, however, our attention needs to turn to the second crack that threatens democratic liberal capitalism: economic mismanagement.

## 3. Economic mismanagement

Economic mismanagement causes much unrest, hardship and anxiety among *the forgotten ones*. A large proportion of the Australian population is deprived of some essential form of economic support and is powerless to do anything about it.

Countless illustrations could be provided to support this argument. For instance, the funding of the aged care sector comes to mind. With the advent of a rapidly ageing population, an ever-increasing level of financial support is required to fund the sector. The Parliamentary Budget Office has estimated that over the present decade, Australian Government spending will increase by 4% per annum, after correcting for inflation. This increase will mean that aged care spending will grow significantly faster than the rate of increase of all other government expenditures. In 2019-20, the amount of government expenditure in aged care already totalled $21.2 billion.[28]

Meanwhile, the incidence of abuse in aged care facilities beggars belief. In the 2021 Final Aged Care Commission Report, we read that 5,718 allegations of assault were made under the

---

[28] https://www.royalcommission.gov.au/system/files/2021-03/final-report-executive-summary.pdf, p3 (accessed 15/11/2023)

Aged Care Act. A further 27,000 to 39,000 also occurred that were exempt from mandatory reporting because they were resident-on-resident incidents.[29]

A government reform agenda is underway, but this is nothing new, and judging by the record of the last 20 years, the jury is still out since little progress has been achieved in spite of numerous reforms undertaken by successive governments of either political persuasion.

To make matters worse, ideological divisions retard progress. For instance, the royal commissioners in charge of the disability Royal Commission still cannot agree on a uniform set of recommendations. As a result, the Albanese government has *"kicked the idea of a new disability rights act, the first recommendation, down the road, saying it would be part of a broader discussion about whether Australia should adopt a human rights Act"*.[30]

How is it, then, that the voice of this significant proportion of the population is not being heard? How is it that the major political parties of either persuasion are not responding to the vociferous complaints of their voters? How do the major parties manage to receive sufficient support at the ballot box to gain re-election in the light of such a poor performance?

This is one of the questions this book is attempting to address but before doing so, it is important to understand what is at the root of the macroeconomic mismanagement of the Australian economy.

One of the major causes of economic mismanagement in this country is rent-seeking.

Rent-seeking is an economic concept that occurs when an entity seeks to gain added wealth without any reciprocal

---

[29] https://www.royalcommission.gov.au/system/files/2021-03/final-report-executive-summary.pdf, p.8 (accessed 15/1/2023)

[30] Lunn Stephen, *Ideological divisions knock wind out of disability reform, The Weekend Australian, August 3-4 2024, p.19*

contribution of productivity. Typically, it revolves around government-funded social services and social service programs.[31]

The benefit of rent-seeking practices in Australia accrues to the bureaucracy – in other words, to the public service, the government departments and the institutions controlled either by Canberra or the individual federated States.

One of the most striking examples of rent-seeking in Australia is the amended Closing the Gap Agreement that was signed by the Commonwealth, State and Territories in 2020. The new Agreement was expected to remedy the failures of the previous one, where only two of the twelve targets had been met.

The key pillars of the revised Agreement revolve around four priority reforms:

1) formal partnerships and shared decisions making;
2) building the community-controlled sector,
3) transforming government organisations and
4) shared access to date and information at a regiona. level.

In themselves, these reform areas would appear to resonate with the concerns most people have about the state of the Aboriginal Affairs administration: inefficient bureaucracy, poor administrative controls and little or no proper accountability.

However, a review published by the Productivity Commission in 2023 reveals that launching the amended Agreement seems to be another exercise in virtue signalling – in other words, being seen as doing the "right thing" with no real serious intention to make any change.

In the first paragraphs of its Executive Summary, the draft review report states the following:

---

[31] https://www.investopedia.com/terms/r/rentseeking.asp#toc-what-is-rent-seeking

*"The Productivity Commission's first review of the Agreement shows that governments are not adequately delivering on this commitment. Progress in implementing the Agreement's Priority Reforms has, for the most part, been weak and reflects a business-as-usual approach to implementing policies and programs that affect the lives of Aboriginal and Torres Strait Islander people. Current implementation raises questions about whether governments have fully grasped the scale of change required...it is too easy to find examples of government decisions that contradict commitments in the Agreement, that do not reflect Aboriginal and Torres Strait Islander people's priorities and perspectives and that exacerbate rather than remedy, disadvantage and discrimination... Without strong accountability for its implementation across all government organisations, the Agreement risks becoming another broken promise to Aboriginal and Torres Strait Islander people."*[32]

Further on, the Report also states:

*"There is, for the most part, no strategic approach that explains (and provides evidence) how the initiatives that governments have identified will achieve the fundamental transformation envisaged in the Agreement. This makes it near impossible for the Aboriginal and Torres Strait Islander people, and the broader Australian community, to use the plans to hold governments to account".*

---

[32] Productivity Commission, Review of the National Agreement on Closing the Gap Draft Report, Canberra, July 2023.

*It would thus seem that very little to no concern is expressed at government level about the astronomical cost incurred in maintaining offices dealing with Aboriginal Affairs in Australia which, already in 2016, was estimated to be $33.4 billion per annum.[33]*

We have cited aged care and aboriginal affairs as strong examples of government economic mismanagement of our economy. There are others but in most, if not all cases, the root cause lies in a lack of accountability brought about by poor management and project review practices.

For instance, in the West Australian Auditor General 2023 Major Project Transparency report, we read the following:

*"For the 20 projects we reviewed, cost budgets have increased by almost $2 billion (22.5%) since their original approval, from a total of $8.7 billion to $10.7 billion. Most have either received more funding and/or had their completion dates extended. About 50% of this $2 billion increase was approved recently as part of the 2023-24 Budget process and is largely related to three rail/road projects".*

*"Fifteen projects had their prior approved cost and/or time budgets increased during the 2022-23 Mid-Year Review and 2023-24 Budget processes…*

*"We note that five projects highlighted in our 2022 Transparency Report as having had high variations to either their cost and/or time continued to experience*

---

[33] Steering Committee for the Review of Government Service Provision (2017). *2017 Indigenous Expenditure Report,* Commonwealth Productivity Commission, xii, cited by Gary Johns, *The Burden of Culture,* Quadrant Books 2022, p.84. The report specifies that on an individual basis, this is about twice the amount spent on non-Aboriginal Australians.

*increases."[34]*

It is also worth noting that in November 2023, the Federal Labor Government announced its decision to axe 50 projects from the Commonwealth $120bn capital works pipeline due to spiralling costs and runway delays.[35]

Finally, there is the report of the Auditor General in the financial management of the COVID pandemic in Western Australia, which informs us that $580 million were spent on the pandemic without clear evidence of the necessity for it. This led the Auditor General to conclude his report in these words:

> *'I acknowledge the uncertainty that the pandemic created...however, I have never before witnessed such escalation in the cost of a program over such a short timeframe, occurring with a lack of due consideration of the impacts, or without a record of anyone pausing to ask what level of procurement was sufficient and whether this had been achieved.'[36]*

More case studies and illustrations could be provided but it is clear that the various examples of economic mismanagement we pointed out so far can only lead us to one inescapable major conclusion: government budgetary expenditure control appears to be a problem.

The question is: why?

The answer is that little to no attention is paid to performance benchmarks. The focus is not on service delivery and

---

[34] https://audit.wa.gov.au/reports-and-publications/reports/2023-transparency-report-major-projects (accessed 16 November 2023)
[35] "50 road and rail projects cancelled from nation's $120 bn infrastructure pipeline" The Australian, 16 November 2023
[36] https://audit.wa.gov.au/wp-content/uploads/2023/05/Media-statement-FA-State-Government-2021-22-Part-2-COVID-19-Impacts.pdf (extracted 09/04/2024

performance but on ideology, in other words, on propaganda.

The reason for this is because our governments are pandering to key centres of influence, to those who have progressively infiltrated our institutions and who, thanks partly to the Internet and social media, can broadcast their messages so loudly as to impact on the vote at the ballot box. Expressed differently, our governments are not unlike parents who have become fearful of their children – children who suffer from behavioural problems that parents do not know how to tackle. Eventually, these parents capitulate and give in to their children, yielding to their tantrums; they give them the objects of their desire without much consideration of the cost involved.

Emotional ideology now drives politics. The screaming "teals" are exerting more influence on the political scene, and consequently, the major parties, in an attempt to placate them, want to be all things to all men and women.

It would seem that where the ideology winds lead us does not matter, as long as the government is re-elected, as long as the so-called elites retain their power.

Indeed, it would be foolish to think that governments are elected on their economic credentials.

"It's the economy, stupid" was a phrase coined by James Carville, political adviser to Bill Clinton, in 1992, and although it might have resonated with the electorate at the time, it no longer resonates with our elites, with those that have a major impact on our electoral outcomes. What matters now to governments is what they give to the people, or better still, what the people perceive they are given, not economic performance. This is why countries with budget deficits sustained by excessive indebtedness continue to have the same type of government elected, over and over again.

However, in a country such as Australia, where 97% of the working-age population has a paid job, you need, as a rich parent would, offer more than generous monetary allowances to satisfy your children. Governments understand this, and they move towards more intangible and illusionary pursuits, such as woke ideology dictates, irrespective of the costs involved.

The strategy is always the same and starts with a noble lie, for instance, the claim that climate change is such an imminent threat that we are facing extinction in the next twenty to thirty years unless we do something about it now. The experts know this is not true (ask Bjorn Lomborg, for instance), but this is what the screaming, powerful, well-resourced "teals" want to hear, so we spend money on schemes beyond our means; we run deficits we cannot afford but who cares as long as we get re-elected?

Yes, I can hear you say that you, dear reader, and many others are already aware of all of this, but this is the whole point: you are aware of it and many others are aware of it! A significant portion of the general public is aware of it, and in view of the numbers involved, not only significant resentment is experienced, but fear and alienation also.

There is this feeling at the level of the individual that "I don't matter/the government does not care about me/nothing I say or do will make a difference". This is the experience of the forgotten people. We are emotionally manipulated.

Naturally, our Australian governments will not have a bar of this and, therefore, will go to great lengths to "demonstrate" that performance matters.

Indeed, how else could you be re-elected otherwise?

Yet, it is all illusory.

So, we start a new project because we know it will resonate positively with a segment of the voting population we want to reach out to, but once the project is going, little attention is paid as to whether it is delivering the goods and is on budget.

Initial project evaluation is also sadly lacking.

For instance, the Thinktank Committee for Economic Development of Australia (CEDA) found that, out of a sample of 20 Federal Government programs with a total expenditure of more than $200 billion, ninety-five per cent had not been properly evaluated. Its findings reveal that, over the past decade, federal and state government spending has been increasing by roughly 5% each year but has made no difference in reducing poverty and disadvantage.[37]

A strong example of being seen to do the "right thing" is also the AUKUS submarine deal. Its motivation is to reassure our population that national defence issues are being prioritised in the wake of global tensions and an increasingly aggressive Chinese stance.

Yet, as former Foreign Affairs Minister Alexander Downer revealed in a recent press interview, the idea of building submarines in Australia is "a political fantasy".[38] The cost is prohibitive, and the technological complexity is too great. However, it looks good; it sends the message that this will create jobs and will provide a stimulus not only to the local economy but to the nation as a whole. It "feels good" and in postmodern times, if it feels good, do it! In other words, without wishing to put too fine a point on it, a large part of the submarine project is a smokescreen.

Ideology drives everything.

Western Australia's largest integrated electricity generator and energy retailer, Synergy, posted a net loss of $732.6 million in the financial year 2022-2023. This loss performance does not

---

37

https://cedakenticomedia.blob.core.windows.net/cedamediacontainer/ke ntico/media/attachments/ceda-disrupting-disadvantage-3-finding-what-works.pdf (accessed 26/10/2023)
38 Warning on flawed AUKUS subs agenda, Week End Australian, October 28-29 2023

seem to ring any alarm bells with the West Australian government; the trend is well entrenched and accepted as a necessary outlay for a strategy focused on the abandonment of coal. Synergy's net loss was $262 million in 2020/21 and $429 million in 2021/2022. Naturally, this is unsustainable, and just in case the reader still has any doubt about the quality of our government's financial management and accountability, I will cite one last example.

A recent Auditor-General report covering the operations of the Australian Federal Government raised significant concerns about the ethics of Government departments:

> *"Performance audits present strong evidence that public sector ethics, integrity and probity need to be a continuing focus. Ethical findings were explicitly raised in two audits in 2022–23 (Auditor-General Report No. 31 2022–23 Administration of the Community Health and Hospitals Program and Auditor-General Report No. 5 2022–23 Digital Transformation Agency's Procurement of ICT-Related Services) while many others raised issues with the integrity of entity operations, particularly relating to non-compliance with mandatory requirements. In routine areas of public administration, such as meeting record-keeping requirements, performance consistently falls short. In the last five years, the ANAO has made negative comments on record-keeping in over 90 per cent of performance audit reports presented to the Parliament.[39]*

---

[39] https://www.anao.gov.au/work/annual-report/anao-annual-report-2022-23 (accessed 26/10/2023)

This poor economic performance has now started to have wide repercussions, particularly since, at the time of writing this book, the Federal Government and the Reserve Bank have been working against each other. Whilst the Reserve Bank is obsessed with bringing inflation down through the use of monetary policy, the Federal Labor Government is focusing on increasing expenditure to counteract the pain inflicted by higher interest rates.

As leading economist Chris Richardson remarked, we are currently witnessing:

> *"a much bigger fall in living standards than we have seen in any recession in living memory...past recessions have fallen very much on a relatively handful...past falls in living standards were very concentrated...this time many people are getting hit...if you are a wage earner, wages have not kept up with prices; if you are a borrower, interest rates have roared up; if you are a taxpayer, the personal tax rate has risen very fast...the financial pain in Australia has been (sic) accumulated as Covid savings disappear; it hits lower and middle-income people".*[40]

In fact, this state of affairs is now prompting some to ask who is really running Australia? Is it the government? Is it the unions, or is it the activists? Is the country run by the CFMEU or the climate cultists or the anti-Semitics or, as Gemma Tognini recently asked, in the murky waters of a post-truth world, is anyone at the helm of SS Australia? [41]

---

[40] Quoted in "Middle-class woes turn into electoral tidal wave" The Weekend Australian, Dec. 2-3 2023

[41] Tognini Gemma, The Weekend Australin, July 20-21, 2024, p.20.

# Summary

In this chapter, we considered the different types of cracks that have gradually emerged in our Australian democratic edifice.

The common denominator is a feeling of powerlessness and alienation among a significant number of Australians. We have identified globalisation as a major catalyst, not only from an economic perspective but also from a sociological vantage.

We have discovered that economic globalisation brought about by the pursuit of international capitalism has contributed to much insecurity and anxiety among the forgotten people.

It has also heralded the advent of multiculturalism and its offspring: post-nationalism.

The latter continues to prove to be a serious threat to the quality of our Australian democracy. Indeed, whilst multiculturalism might be managed partly through a refinement of our immigration policies, post-nationalism will, by its nature, continue to be a more difficult foe to conquer as it goes to the core of who really governs Australia and what new values are imposed on our society by the global order.

We have also established that the quality of our Australian democracy is significantly compromised through poor economic management. Both Federal and State governments have attracted and continue to attract a significant level of independent audit criticism for the quality of their governance. Projects are started with insufficient consideration of the cost they impose on the Australian population; they are "sold" to voters through emotional propaganda and through a deliberate focus on short-term benefits.

We conclude that, whilst post-nationalism is partly the cause of the apparently unstoppable expansion of a new type of "elite" ideology, economic mismanagement, on the other hand, is the consequence of the obsession placed on the adoption of a set of new values at the expense of good monetary and fiscal governance.

Globalisation and economic performance are two major features of the capitalist system but unfortunately, they now appear to be undermining the very essence of what capitalism sets out to achieve: a sustainable high level of democratic freedom for all people.

# Chapter 3

## Hypocrisy: the Ideological Mantle of the New "Elites"

*"Hypocrisy is the homage vice pays to virtue".*

François de la Rochefoucauld

We have now established that a significant proportion of the Australian population, this subset I have named the genuinely forgotten people, are disillusioned, frustrated and relatively powerless for two main reasons.

Firstly, Australia is part of a new global economy that is heralding the advent of a new world order: post-nationalism. This is perceived by many as a new source of threat to the old-fashioned values on which Australian democracy has thrived and evolved.

Secondly, the genuinely forgotten people are the victims of the poor performance of the bureaucratic echelons and, in particular, of the wasted expenditure of taxpayer money on ill-conceived or unaffordable "pie in the sky" projects.

In contrast, the claiming-to-be-forgotten are not overlooked: they attract an excessive amount of attention from the media and the "elites". Their source of discontent arises from their insatiable appetite for more and more institutional and governmental support.

Yet, both are manipulated, consciously or unconsciously, by a new type of elite class, different from the old bourgeoisie but which, nevertheless, turns out to be a significant source of discontent for both types of forgotten people.

Who are the new "elites"? They are certainly not a unique Australian breed. They exist in most parts of the Western world, but they tend to be located mostly in centres of influence and for that reason, we find many of them in the leading capital cities of the so-called Free World: Paris, London, Brussels, New York, Rome, Munich and the like.

In Australia, their location is more diverse because of our decentralised federal system of government, but it is safe to say that most of them reside in our two largest capital cities, Sydney and Melbourne and of course, in our national capital, Canberra.

As a matter of fact, Canberra is a microcosm of the new "elites".

Canberra boasts a typical elite profile: a median weekly household income higher than the national average; a higher percentage of employment, a higher level of education and a higher degree of atheism. It also offers virtually no rental housing for a couple with two children on the minimum wage. Finally, it is a public service city with 35% of its population employed in the public sector.[42]

Canberra and ACT political allegiances strongly stand left-of-centre. At the time of writing, Labor had won six consecutive elections and had governed in partnership with the Greens since 2012; Canberrans voted for same-sex marriage before the issue was voted on at the national level and overwhelmingly supported the "Yes" case in the recent *Voice* Referendum.

Canberra's economic performance is not as strong as the rest of the nation. Ratings agency Standard & Poors stripped the territory of its AAA credit rating, offering further evidence that performance ranks as a distant second to the propagation of an

---

[42] "Canberra hostile territory: how it compares with the nation; The Week End Australian, October28-29 2023.

ideology that wants to give the vote to 16-year-olds and to see children as young as 12 to be free to change their gender; an ideology that has also banned new gas connections but will mandate electric cars; and an ideology that has led the Australian Capital Territory government to take over the Calvary public hospital (because of its strong Catholic opposition to abortion and euthanasia).[43]

In fact, the more "woke" governments become, the worse their economic performance.

Another example to illustrate the point is Victoria. Under the former leadership of Dan Andrews, the State of Victoria excelled in promoting the cause of the woke movement. Dan Andrews introduced voluntary assisted dying laws, supported abortion on demand, championed the "Safe"(?) Schools initiative, heralded the first "safe" drug injection rooms and supported the right for school students to strike in favour of climate change.

One of its major "achievements" was the *Change or Suppression (Conversion) Practices Prohibition Act 2021*. This Act of Parliament assists gender transitioners but not de transitioners; it does not respect the fact that a person might change his or her mind; it bans all forms of psychological, psychiatric or other therapy intervention, it bans prayers or other religious practices destined to suppress sexual orientation, whether requested or not and it prohibits moving a person outside of Victoria for the purpose of changing or suppressing the sexual orientation or gender identity of the person, whether this is at the request of the person concerned or not.

When so much attention is focused on the implementation of a specific ideology, it is little wonder that economic

---

[43] Woke capital risks leading the rest of the nation to pot; The Weekend Australian, October 28-29 2023.

performance runs a distant last on the ladder of priorities.

It is therefore not surprising that in its 2022-2023 annual financial report, the Auditor General warned that Victoria's State debt will crash through $250bn within four years and that no indication has been provided of when and how the State will be able to start paying down the debt it has and further debt it plans to accumulate.[44]

Alarmingly, Victoria is not alone. At the time of writing this book, much talk is being made about the possibility of downgrading the New South Wales government's credit rating. Furthermore, the 2024 budget of the Queensland government is plunging that State into a 3bn deficit a year after a super-profits tax on coal companies handed Queensland's Labor government the largest surplus in history".[45]

Where does this woke ideology come from? I gave the answer in my previous book, *Silent, Fragile and Isolated*, but it is worth stressing that it is one of the manifestations of post-nationalism impacting Australia.

Hypocrisy is at the core of the woke movement and the hypocrisy of the "elites" knows no geographical boundaries.

In my country of birth, France, it is well entrenched. This was already well documented a few years ago by French sociologist Christophe Guilluy in his book *Le crépuscule de la France d'en haut*, translated into English as *The Twilight of the Elites*.[46]

On page 21, Guilluy writes:

"*In taking up residence in the major European cities*

---

[44] No Plan to cut $256bn State debt; The Weekend Australian, November 25-26 2023.

[45] Lydia Lynch, *Miles empties his state's piggy bank to save Labor,* The Weekend Australian, June 8-9 2024.

[46] The Twilight of the Elites, English translation 2019 Yale University, originally published as Le Crépuscule. de la France d'en haut, Flammarion, Paris 2016

*and the regional centres of France, corporate executives and their counterparts in the academy and the liberal professions consciously or unconsciously endorse a strategy of social ghettoization".*

And on page 22:

*"The upper classes call for equality among the nation's regions while at the same time promoting metropolization and gentrification: they demand greater social diversity but separate themselves from the lower classes by living apart from them; they urge everyone to get along but create a ghettoized educational system in which the children of the poor have no choice but to go to public schools that their own children are able to avoid; they uphold republican principles (and none more resolutely than the principle of equality) but in reality favour inegalitarianism".*

It is, therefore, a display of hypocrisy.

It is not just European snobbery.

In Australia, too, where a more widespread sense of egalitarianism has developed (the Australian "fair go"), we can see that the "elites" do not care much for anyone else than themselves.

The snobbery here is expressed somewhat differently than it is in France, but snobbery it is, nevertheless.

France covers an area of approximately 550,000 square kilometres, Australia boasts 7.6 million square kilometres. Whilst the snobbery of the "elites" in France is better highlighted by their insistence on taking refuge in a minuscule portion of the already small French territory – Paris – in Australia, their snobbery is more visibly displayed, not so much geographically, in spite of my earlier comments about Canberra, but rather by the insistence of their virtue signalling.

Much talk is made of the "gap" between white and black in Australia but no concrete measures are taken that will make a difference.

For instance, had the *Voice* referendum found a place in our Constitution, nothing would have changed apart from more speeches, more debates and more money finding its way, not to the areas where squalor really prevails, but mostly in the pockets of a greedy administration, made up of both whites and a number of privileged blacks.

Even this presumed champion of the new woke diversity, the Australian Broadcasting Corporation has been proven to be a first-class hypocrite. In the recent Listen Loudly, Act Strongly review, the independent inquirers found that out of 120 participants, comprising past and present employees, only one described not experiencing racism in the workplace personally. Racial slurs, derogatory comments, stereotyping and bias were reported to be commonplace.[47]

The "elites" speak much about saving the planet, but they fly in expensive private jets that consume much fuel to meet in the highly exclusive Swiss mountain resort of Davos. Even more outrageous was the number of attendees at the IPCC's CoP 28 meeting in Dubai where no less than 97,372 persons were registered for on-site attendance.[48]

The "elites" voice their support for diversity but, in practice, support exclusivity. They only want one type of society, with one mindset, one where woke triumphalism is obsessively feted in all spheres of life, in all circumstances, with utmost fervour, leaving

---

[47] Listen Loudly, Act Strongly, Independent Review into ABC Systems and Processes in Support of Staff who Experience Racism, 2024, https://live-production.wcms.abc-cdn.net.au/726cda3b8b2694cd1714c3c5ada5254c, accessed 03/10/2024

[48] https://enb.iisd.org/united-arab-emirates-climate-change-conference-cop28-summary

no room for dissension, no place for free speech, no existence for Christian schools, no tolerance for a different voice, but just the senseless mantra of the uniform message emanating from the sadness of their echo chambers.

The real power of the "elites" is that they occupy all our society's key centres of influence: the educational sector, the courts, the legislative chambers and most importantly, the media.

It is essential for the "elites" that they do not appear to be domineering, to be imposing. Indeed, they need to pretend to be egalitarian to gather sufficient support for their ill-conceived good causes and mostly they have succeeded in doing so.

They have made a clean break from the old European bourgeoisie, they are the "bohemian bourgeois" the "bobos" as the French call them, not the nobility, not the aristocracy, not even the upper middle class of the 19th and 20th centuries.

The old Australian bourgeoise, the "old money", was mostly found in the upper echelons of the Melburnian and Sydneysider society. As was the case for its European "cousin", the old Australian bourgeoisie, endowed with its English heritage, was not shy in separating itself from the rest of society. Consequently, it could afford to be ostentatious, for its self-segregation provided a mantle of anonymity from the wider public gaze.

By contrast, today's new "elites" promote a type of diversity where they need to be seen and upheld as the new paragons of virtue, constantly sending a message of false humility, false repentance and fabricated guilt. Although they do not wish to be seen to belong to the high society, they are happy to adopt a high profile because of their misplaced "missionary zeal" and the fact that their positions in society are so much in the public eye: High Court judges, university professors, famous writers, well-known actors and artists, leading editors and media commentators.

If the old bourgeoisie could dominate economically and, in some cases, exploit an unfortunate proletariat, today's "bobo" wants to appear to be one of us and, for this purpose, addresses the rest of us more unfortunate plebeians, in a language loaded with emotional overtones because emotions can bind people together in a way that the intellect cannot ever achieve.

Furthermore, in spite of wanting to appear to be just one of us, the new "bobo" suffers from a high complex of intellectual superiority. They are the ones who have the benefit of a university education which makes them think that they know best and that we, mere mortals, could not possibly understand the complexity of world affairs. They do not explain, not so much because they do not understand, but because they think facts and explanations are beyond the intelligence of the average voter. "Trust us", they say, "we are the new Gnostics; we have the special insight, the understanding of the new morality which we offer to the world as salvation from the so-called misdeeds of the past".

Gerard Henderson calls them the "modern-day revolutionaries". He writes that they *"are embarrassed by their wealth but not to the extent of giving it up or handing over their property to the dispossessed."* In an oblique reference to the opening of the 2024 Olympic Games in Paris, he also adds: *"it is easier to mock Christianity and bemoan Western civilisation while receiving handouts from taxpayers to perform on the river Seine to the applause of the left intelligentsia".*[49]

---

[49] Henderson Gerard "Sneering attacks from left elite eat away at West's score", The Weekend Australian, August 3-4 2024, p.15

# Summary

A numerous, frustrated, disillusioned class of people is overlooked by a growing minority of "elites" who occupy positions of influence in most, if not all, countries with Western European cultural heritage.

In Australia, they are found principally in our capital cities but particularly more so in Canberra. They are different from the bourgeois ruling classes of the 19th and early mid-20th centuries: they adopt a higher social profile, keen to maximise visibility in order to pursue their passion for cultural change. They excel in virtue signalling but achieve little that is positive; they decry the circumstances of the so-called oppressed but provide no real remedy to the malaise they claim to diagnose.

In Australia, the State of Victoria and the Australian Capital Territory (ACT) are the epitome of the woke elite movement. Every government policy is imbued with woke ideology which takes priority over all areas; economic performance is therefore relegated to a distant last priority. The ACT economic rating has been downgraded and the debt of the State of Victoria has now been predicted to exceed $250 billion soon.

Nevertheless, few in the upper government echelons appear to be concerned by this state of affairs. Instead, a culture of economic complacency and intellectual condescending superiority continues to abound among those who, endowed with the so-called benefits of a tertiary education, think they know better than their forgotten "subjects".

# Chapter 4

## The New Virtues

*"The greatest minds are capable of the greatest vices as well as of the greatest virtues".*

(René Descartes)

The artillery of the "elites" comprises a number of effective weapons which reflect, in turn, the new 21st century "virtues": authenticity, empathy, humility, self-care and vulnerability. (I am indebted to Lucinda Holdforth for pointing these out in her short monograph *21st Century Virtues: How They are Failing our Democracy.)*[50]

To these, I will add outrage, fear, guilt, envy and love.

Some of these, such as empathy, humility and love would seem to fall into the categories of commonly recognised virtues and therefore cause no contention. Others, such as self-care, fear, guilt and envy appear to be out of place among traditional moral values.

This is because the woke movement is radically different from anything that has preceded it. The words it uses do not have the same definitions we have traditionally ascribed to them.

The woke movement is immersed in emotions. Most of the words it uses carry emotional connotations; woke philosophy has re-invented a new emotional language and our non-elected

---

[50] Lucinda Holdforth; 21st century virtues: how they are failing our democracy; Monash University Publishing, 2023.

"elites" are increasingly resorting to the use of emotions to impose a type of nefarious ideology which influences the outcome of many of our elections.

Let us therefore spend some time looking at the meaning of these new "virtuous" emotions.

- ### Love

Until recently, most people would have best defined love as C.S Lewis did, that is to say in four categories comprising some or all of the following features: empathy (storge), friendship (philia), romance and sexual love (eros) and unconditional love (agape).

Unfortunately, the woke culture's definition of love does not fit into these traditionally accepted categories.

The woke love fails on empathy because a prerequisite for empathy is support for human dignity.

The woke "elites" claim that they support human dignity by upholding diversity but their actions are actually demeaning and humiliating.

They demonstrate a serious lack of emotional intelligence, another prerequisite to any claim of empathy.

Take, for instance, the issue of euthanasia.

Proponents of euthanasia seek to justify their position by saying that they wish to preserve human dignity.

They show great emotional turmoil at the thought that some might die in great pain, and they ask what dignity is there in allowing people to die in circumstances when we would not allow a dog to live. Yet, they lack the emotional intelligence to ask the follow-up question: what dignity is there in death? Particularly, if death is the end of everything, if there is nothing beyond the tomb or the ashes, apart from some romantic idea of the spirit of the departed watching over us?

They seem to lack the emotional intelligence to ask why we allow euthanasia to take place in cases of chronic pain for the terminally ill with less than six months to live. Why not kill everyone in chronic pain whether terminally ill or not? Why six months? Why only allow those who can express their wishes clearly to select the exit option? What about the mentally deficient, the young child etc.?

If you google 'emotional intelligence', you may read that emotional intelligence has the following attributes:

*"Self-management – You're able to control impulsive feelings and behaviours, manage your emotions in healthy ways, take initiative, follow through on commitments, and adapt to changing circumstances.*

*Self-awareness – You recognise your own emotions and how they affect your thoughts and behaviour. You know your strengths and weaknesses and have self-confidence.*

*Social awareness – You have empathy. You can understand the emotions, needs, and concerns of other people, pick up on emotional cues, feel comfortable socially, and recognise the power dynamics in a group or organisation.*

*Relationship management – You know how to develop and maintain good relationships, communicate clearly, inspire and influence others, work well in a team, and manage conflict*[i]*".*

Woke philosophy is deficient on each of these counts.

It fails on self-management as it cannot control impulsive feelings and behaviours which categorise people on the basis of the colour of their skin. White is bad, black is good. Black lives matter, white lives matter less, if at all.

It fails on self-awareness as it does not realise (or does not care) that the outrage it expresses in condemning all aspects of Western thought and civilisation is actually an expression of the racist nature this same woke philosophy claims to oppose.

It fails on social awareness as it fails to have compassion towards those who fall outside the particular identities approved by the woke "elites".

It fails on relationship management as it perpetuates the very class conflict it claims to oppose.

The woke definition of love also fails with regard to upholding friendship.

Indeed, whilst the woke "elites" are very adept at pretending that they will befriend the so-called vulnerable, they are only interested in imposing their own set of "values". They are not interested in entering into a friendly dialogue with anyone who happens to hold a different opinion than theirs. The woke friendship is a friendship that is based on your accepting their opinions, their values, but not on a reciprocal basis. It is a one-way street friendship, in other words, not friendship at all.

Does the woke love correspond to a traditional definition of romantic love? Not, if you understand "Eros" as being more than self-centred sexual intercourse. Properly understood, romantic love is not self-centred; it is highly emotional and highly centred on the object of one's affections. The 19th-century Romantic poetry focused on the need to be in the presence of the person loved. Romantic love includes passion that results in a deep intimacy that is not merely confined to sexual intercourse but extends to a deep interest in the other person. Romantic lovers have long conversations with each other, they share their joys, victories, failures, doubts, and sufferings.

There is nothing romantic about wokeism: it is self-centred. It is only interested in its own opinions and its ideology; it does not listen; it only engages in monologue and refuses any dialogue that does not mirror its own views.

Having failed on empathy, friendship, romance and unconditional love, how can the woke movement then claim to be a philosophy of love?

Only because of its insistence that it is the very antithesis of "hatred".

The woke movement majors on describing all of its opponents as hateful beings. "If you do not agree with me, it means you hate me."

Love is unconditional acceptance on your part of all of my opinions, not just at the intellectual assent level but also at a celebratory level where you demonstrate by your actions that you are really one of us.

You do not just vote "yes" to a new definition of marriage, you have to celebrate it, attend the annual "gay" parades, participate actively in them, not just cast a blind eye to them.

There is no room for indifference, you have to endorse, and even celebrate, all I stand for and live it to the full. In other words, you can never be woke unless you worship everything that is woke.

The woke movement is not love, it is idolatry.

- **Authenticity**

The woke movement claims to be authentic, in other words, genuine or true, but that is incorrect.

The search for the authentic was the rallying cry of a French philosophical movement led by the likes of Jean Paul Sartre and Simone de Beauvoir in the 1950s and 1960s but it failed to find the truth; it failed to define the essence of what is genuine existence and the movement came to a standstill when Paris Sorbonne's Michel Foucault developed a new theory of knowledge.

Foucault's understanding of knowledge was based on an appreciation of the concept of power. For Foucault, power was everywhere. It prevailed in everything and, therefore, in language. According to him, the power of language or discourse is found in the cultural background of the speaker and the knowledge element that discourse contains is never absolute because the relativism of culture influences it.

So, according to Foucault, nobody knows what is authentic or true because a person's views of what it is results from the influence of the culture in which that person lives or has been brought up. Consequently, everything is blurred and this is how our society can now claim that gender is fluid, that it is not fixed at birth and that it can change over a person's lifetime.

If this were true, this would signify that there cannot be any authenticity in politics.

What is good, what is fair, and what is democratic can no longer be defined by a majority poll, let alone by a political party or a government, because any opinion held is only a cultural construct, the result of a combination of circumstances, colour, education and standing position in society.

Since nothing can be really authentic anymore, everything is therefore inauthentic. There is no rule book, no guide, no set of rules. Worse still, no one can claim that something is false because what is false cannot exist or be defined in the absence of what is right and true.

False is the opposite of true, but if truth is relative, nobody can say that something is absolutely false; falsity then becomes what you decide is not true.

Yet, if this is correct, how can we say that authenticity is one of the 21st-century virtues? How can you make a virtue of something that does not exist?

This is because, together with the other new 21st-century virtues, authenticity is self-referential. As Holdforth explains in her work cited above, prior civilisations developed a set of values, not circling back to the individual's state of being, but rather to external benchmarks, for instance, courage, order and vigour in the Ancient Roman times and ritual, respect and education in the Confucian Chinese model.

*"The distinctive virtues prized by these civilisations shaped their cultures and underpinned their greatest achievements (but) what qualities do we value in today's advanced democratic societies? It seems to me that we prize individual uniqueness, personal experiences of reality and the quest for self-acceptance and self-love".*[51]

The "elites" will insist that there is no democracy without authenticity. Yet, such a bold claim is hypocritical on their part. The "elites" have destroyed authenticity and made everything fluid, changeable and relative. We are asked to be authentic in the way we cast our vote at the ballot box, but those we demand this do not and no longer can do as they preach.

## • Humility

What is humility? According to the Cambridge dictionary, humility is *"the feeling or attitude that you have no special importance that makes you better than others; lack of pride".*

Humility is a key virtue in the woke movement because of its core belief that white people have introduced privilege, supremacy and complicity. In other words: racism.

The woke "elites" feel obligated to preach their own version of a gospel of humility because they believe that everyone but they have failed to pass the test of humility.

In their eyes, if we are white, we cannot be humble, which then makes it difficult to comprehend how they, white themselves, can claim to be what they preach.

There is also a further problem: although humility is indeed incompatible with racism, the woke movement promotes pride. The most obvious example is the annual "Pride" parades in our capital cities and the increasing attendance of our "elites" to each

---

[51] Holdforth (2023), p 3.

of these events.

Likewise, the woke business community also displays a complete lack of humility. These corporate leaders think they know best for they have now "progressed" beyond working for the benefit of their customers and shareholders. They are now more enlightened and understand the importance of promoting an environmental, social and corporate governance agenda (shortened usually as "ESG") at all their annual general meetings, board meetings and summits.

As a matter of fact, more than twenty years ago already, in the year 2000, the United Nations invited a large number of world-leading financial institutions to research and develop a number of recommendations as to how to "integrate environmental, social and governance issues in asset management, securities brokerage services and associated research functions".[52]

Since then, the ESG "religion" has expanded exponentially. A vivid example of this phenomenon in Australia would be the performance of Qantas under the tarnished leadership of their former CEO, Alan Joyce.

Alan Joyce nearly caused the financial demise of Qantas; he also brought about a shareholder revolt provoked by the outrageous level of remuneration proposed for the board of directors, mass employee protests and customer revolts regarding the absence of refunds for flights cancelled during the COVID pandemic.

But Qantas is not an isolated example of corporate delinquency.

---

[52] The Global Compact, Who Cares Wins, Connecting financial Markets to a Changing World, 2004, United Nations
https://www.unepfi.org/fileadmin/events/2004/stocks/who_cares_wins_gl
obal_compact_2004.pdf (sourced 11/12/2023)

As pointed out by Public Discourse, the Journal of the Witherspoon Institute:

> *"the 2004 United Nations report's abstractions have translated into the politicization of every aspect of business: "E" now stands in for climate alarmism that damages energy industries; "S" for pro-abortion and gender ideology; and "G" for decisions on hiring, firing and compensation tied to critical race theory. Today major investment firms grade companies based on their ESG policies, which means that activist notions relating to "environmental justice" and "racial equity" are significantly influencing business decisions. This…pressure(s) companies into elevating social justice grievances over making profit".[53]*

- **Self-care**

The reader might be surprised to see "self-care" listed as a virtue, next to humility. After all, is not humility displayed in the renouncing of the self?

It would seem at least that the Apostle Paul believed so when he wrote these words to the church of Phillippi:

> *"Have this mind among yourselves which is yours in Christ Jesus, who, though he was in the form of God, did not count equality with God a thing to be grasped, but emptied himself, by taking the form of a servant, being born in the likeness of men".[54]*

However, logic and consistency are no hurdles for the woke "elites", and it is not difficult to list self-care as one of the new

---

[53] https://www.thepublicdiscourse.com/2023/02/87247/ (sourced 11/12/2023)
[54] The Holy Bible, Philippians 2, English Standard Version, Text Edition 2016, Crossway.

21st-century virtues since the so-called ethos of wokeism is thoroughly self-referential.

What do the "elites" then mean by self-care?

This is a very challenging question to answer. Whilst the woke ideology will preach the importance of self-denial in order to atone for the "abuse" perpetrated against the Other (aka the black, the LGBTQ+ etc), it also stresses the importance of individual rights for those it considers oppressed.

Self-denial and individual rights thus become some sort of strange bedfellows in wokeism.

Humility and self-sacrifice are reserved for the white. The exhortation reserved for the white is shame, guilt and repentance. For the black and other so-called oppressed categories, it is pride and self-care.

In wokeism, self-care essentially involves the imposition of perceived rights, irrespective of the consequences on others. For example, transgender biological males competing in female sports. No thought is given to the fact that this is unfair and that it makes a mockery of any pretence of equal opportunity.

For this reason, it is not surprising that the woke brand of self-care supports what it considers to be justifiable aggression. The woke "elites" believe that in order to care for oneself, payback must take place. This is not reconciliation, it is retribution.

Does this portray some sort of masochistic tendency since the "elites" are in great proportion white? Not at all! Aggression is justified only against those who have not joined the woke cult.

## • Vulnerability

> *"Every single well-intended thing has been an effort to mollify or provide a level of comfort. Your capacity to be uncomfortable is everything and that's what we*

*have taken from kids. And as a result, we've in many cases, I think, created the exact opposite of what we hope to have: a resilient, sceptical, curious, open-minded, good-natured soul. What we get are fragile, vindictive, accusatory, precious and delicate people. It's crazy to blame them for that because those things have to be taught".*

(The Dad Edge)[55]

Vulnerability is fashionable in our 21st century. The woke "elites" preach the importance of coming to terms with one's vulnerability.

In other words, do not be shy to declare to the whole world:

"I am white; therefore, I am vulnerable to being an oppressor; I am a Christian; therefore, I am vulnerable to being narrow-minded; I am male; therefore, I am vulnerable to being abusive; I am vulnerable to acting in accordance with this oppressive, aggressive, imperialistic nature of mine. Therefore, I declare that I am vulnerable, tempted by my vulnerability and this is my act of public repentance".

Coming to terms with one's vulnerability is also highly recommended to the oppressed; in that case, of course, not as a public act of repentance but as a proud declaration of one's authenticity. This is the coming out of the closet, asserting one's authenticity at the risk of being vilified, maligned and abused by the Other (aka, the middle-aged white Christian politically conservative heterosexual).

One major problem: this so-called virtue is antithetical to free speech and, therefore, to democracy. Indeed, as a highly vulnerable, oppressed person, I am very sensitive to criticism,

---

55 https://www.thepost.on.ca/news/local-news/feeling-isnt-thinking accessed 17/07/2024

and therefore, it is of the utmost importance that no white Christian heterosexual male airs his imperialistic, hateful views of my authenticity!

So, whilst I, an oppressed person, am entitled to air my views, my fears, and my so-called vulnerability, you, being the oppressor, no longer have this privilege.

We are silenced unless we agree we are fearful of voicing our thoughts and we have become increasingly sensitive to what others say or think of us.

We are indeed a vulnerable generation.

Vulnerable to manipulation and therefore to democracy being undermined.

- **Fear**

To the extent that morality defines good and immorality bad, fear is now part of the new morality because it is considered good to be fearful.

Fear is good because by expressing it, you point out that you are on the side of the oppressed.

Fear has become part of the weaponry of anti-democratic politics; for instance, at the World Economic Forum in Davos, Greta Thunberg warned the global leaders:

*"I don't want you to be hopeful. I want you to panic. I want you to feel the fear I feel every day. And then I want you to act. I want you to act as you would in a crisis. I want you to act as if the house was on fire".*[56]

With the demise of intellectual thought and the rise of emotional thinking, fear has indeed become a power tool in the hands of the so-called "elites" to manipulate the hearts and minds of many Australians.

---

[56] Quoted in Silent, Fragile and Isolated, Philippe Jaquenod, p.71, Linellen Press, 2022.

This occurs in two ways: firstly, there is the fear felt by the description of apocalyptic scenarios à la Thunberg, and secondly, there is the fear that if I dare to offer a different point of view, I will be "cancelled", that is rejected, victimised, ridiculed and isolated or accused of not caring about people, the environment etc.

Furthermore, for democracy to be harmed, it matters not which type of fear is experienced. Either type is a powerful influencer in manipulating public opinion.

Indeed, if you are a claim-to-be-forgotten type and you display the apocalyptic fear the "elites" want you to experience, you might act in a different way than you would have had you been able to assess and digest the facts of the situation in a calm and considered way. Likewise, if you are the genuinely forgotten type and you have already been isolated or cancelled by your peers, you might still vote the way your intellect tells you, but you will be fearful of expressing your opinion publicly.

If we accept that democracy is much more than casting a vote at the ballot box, if we accept that a vibrant democracy assumes the free expression of private opinions in the public sphere, then fear, whatever your motives, is now an enemy of democracy.

In the hands of the "elites", fear can influence the behaviour and speech of all voters, whether on the left or on the right of centre. When it comes to complicated issues, such as that posed by Brexit a few years ago, it is much easier for governments to win the popular war by focusing on emotions rather than on logic. Both sides use it. The fear of losing your nation's sovereignty to Brussels was played out by the pro-exit camp and the fear of economic devastation upon exiting the Union was played by the pro-EU forces.

## • Outrage

Outrage is a virtue in the 21st century. We are told that it is good to experience outrage because the emotion proves that we are not indifferent to evil. Viewed from that angle, few would have a problem with outrage. Did not, in fact, Jesus himself display outrage when he overturned the tables of the money changers in the temple in Jerusalem?

The problem nowadays is that what we consider to be outrageous is often what previous generations considered to be good. For instance, nowadays many would think it outrageous that some people can still be religious. This is so because we live now under a new atheism. In the past, atheism was simply a conviction that God does not exist. There was no moral judgment attached to that philosophy. The 'God-is-dead' movement was largely comprised of philosophers who simply believed that God does not exist. Darwin, in his famous book, *The Origins of the Species,* made the case for evolution and opposed anyone who believed in a Divine Creator. His work was further developed by others who offered a variety of explanations, such as the Big Bang Theory, but, until the latter part of the 20th century, atheism remained a philosophical position largely devoid of moral judgement on the so-called religious naïve.

With the rise of the New Atheists, all this started to change. The New Atheists believe that all religion (maybe with the exception of Buddhism) is inimical to happiness and freedom of thought and expression. Largely due to the influence of this new type of "elites" (Richard Dawkins et al), we have been told that it is good to display outrage towards the expression of any religious practice, but more particularly Christianity and

Judaism.[57]

Outrage is nevertheless directed against many other ways of life, practices and beliefs than just religious freedom. We have for instance, the example of outrage displayed against those who do not endorse the net zero emissions diktat. Furthermore, outrage takes many forms, so many in fact that we run the risk of no longer being able to perceive it.

Outrage is so prevalent that it is starting to be normalised. A group of academic researchers identified thirteen types of speech and behaviour that constitute outrage, including insulting language, name-calling, emotional display, verbal fighting, character assassination, misrepresented exaggeration, mockery, conflagration, ideological extremism language, belittling and obscene language. They also came to the conclusion that there is such a thing as an outrage industry and that it is thriving economically.[58]

Expressions of outrage may be found in our newspapers, particularly those on the left-of-centre, such as the *Guardian*, among lobby groups and on current affairs programs such as The Drum, Q & A and Media Watch, which, by the way, are all ABC taxpayer-funded productions.

There are also radio talkback shows boasting highly popular hosts, as well as countless podcasts and blogs.

Social media is, of course, the most accessible forum to read or write outrage. Facebook, Instagram, and Twitter are vehicles of choice to vent one's anger, resentment and hatred.[59]

---

[57] Fortunately, this is now starting to change. A new generation of public intellectuals (Douglas Murray, Jordan Petersen etc), still sceptical of the Christian faith, are nevertheless considering the moral virtues expounded in the New Testament Bible.

[58] Berry J & Sobieraj S, The Outrage Industry, Political Opinion Media & the New Incivility, Oxford University Press, 2014

[59] Facebook, of course, does not look for context but simply for words. A friend of mine told me that an apology for mistyping a particular word,

Outrage and anger are particularly prevalent in the United States. In fact, some have argued that in that country, "anger and rage have been institutionalised and are now a continuing feature of the polarised political system".[60] Although it might be somewhat premature to make a similar pronouncement in the case of Australia, we are certainly travelling in the same direction and will eventually reach the same destination, unless we soon choose to turn around.

Outrage is influential. It arouses emotions and strong feelings; it creates guilt and resentment and, once perpetrated on a large scale, it results in a breakdown of peace and order. It is at the root of revolutionary movements. Democracy and political outrage are not compatible because political outrage results in anger and thus endeavours to impose by force a way of life, a specific worldview and diktat without regard to the well-being and rights of all.

- **Envy**

Envy is what drives Marxist philosophy. The old economic Marxism, pitting the proletariat against the "domination" of the capitalists, was already fuelled by envy. Since wokeism is a cultural form of Marxism, it is not surprising that envy features at the core of the movement.

Envy is not the same as jealousy.

Jealousy is the resentment of your having access to something that is mine; for instance, a jealous spouse resents that the

---

rendered as "my stupid big fat fingers" was deleted for using the offensive words "stupid", "big" and "fat". Furthermore, Facebook seems to object to both positive and negative comments and the same friend told me that her expression "As usual, beautifully written, and well researched" was withdrawn on the grounds that it was intentionally courting for excessive "likes".

[60] Cloninger S.C& Leibo S, Understanding Angry Groups, Praeger, Santa Barbara, 2017, p.241.

affection of her husband is shared with a third party.

Envy, on the other hand, is resenting someone else's access to something I do not have.

Woke philosophy is the philosophy of envy because it encourages certain types of persons to resent not having the recognition others might have or not having the same standard of living others enjoy.

In fact, envy is nothing short of coveting.

Envy is the emotion that drives the distributive justice movement.

Distributive justice is not meritorious.

According to distributive justice, or communism, everybody should be entitled to the same benefits. There is no prize for effort. Efforts or merit are not to be rewarded because, apparently, everyone is entitled to the same privileges. What you put in and what you contribute should not determine what you receive.

Why? Because, according to distributive justice, outcomes reflect birth privileges, that is, the cultural background to which you have been exposed, in other words, Michel Foucault's theory of power which, among other things, is expressed in language. According to distributive justice, it is unfair to reward the so-called meritorious because he really has no such merits. He or she simply retains an unfair advantage arising from a more privileged background, dictated in turn by the chance of being born, for instance, white or male or heterosexual.

Woke philosophy is full of contradictions: as we have seen earlier on, it claims to promote human dignity but has no empathy; it claims to promote love but actually foments hatred, so it is not altogether surprising that it makes envy a virtue and simultaneously aims to eradicate it from culture.

The aim of woke philosophy is communism, no class distinctions, no reward for effort, everyone enjoying the same outcome, nobody having more, no one having less. According to this utopian (or rather dystopian?) dream, there is no room for envy. I cannot envy you if you have exactly the same "privileges" that I have. Consequently, it is fair to say that the woke movement is working towards the elimination of envy in our society.

Yet, curiously, illogically, it promotes it as a virtue.

For the woke person, envy is a virtue because it is the fuel that drives the culture war in which it is engaged.

The woke world is made up of two major classes of persons: the oppressor and the oppressed.

In a curious way, the oppressed are encouraged to be envious of the oppressor.

Not in the sense of taking on their persona, so to speak, but rather envious of the privileges that the so-called oppressor has over them. The woke person, therefore, wants to snatch the privileges of the oppressor and appropriates them to himself.

In other words, for the woke individual, it is good to be envious because without envy there is no incentive to destroy the oppressor.

## • Guilt

What about guilt? It is at the core, the very essence of the woke movement. How can guilt be a virtue?

Guilt precedes repentance.

Before I can repent of any wrongdoing I have committed, I need to feel guilty for my action.

Guilt implies the recognition that something I did was not good, not moral, not wholesome.

Once, I have recognised this, once I have appropriated a sense of guilt to my own action, I can then move on to the next stage: repentance.

Indeed, repentance involves a renunciation of my past

actions; it is not just feeling sorry about what I did but rather it is a determination of not doing it again; it is a turning of the way. In that sense, repentance is not necessarily just an action reserved for persons of faith (e.g. Christians) and although the word is hardly used outside Christian circles, the concept it embodies is applicable to all persons who want to change their course of action.

It follows, therefore, that guilt can only disappear once repentance has occurred AND once guilt has been paid for. This is the principle of restitutionary justice where the victim is fully compensated for the wrongdoing that has been committed.

The woke "elites" do not believe that repentance is possible. They argue that once white, always white, once an oppressor, always an oppressor. We are conditioned to remain oppressors because we are the product of our imperialistic culture. Furthermore, we cannot provide proper restitution because we would not know how to do it, so we are condemned to virtue signalling.

Yes, this is a very depressing ideology, a very negative worldview, so once again, how can guilt be made a virtue?

In woke philosophy, guilt is elevated to virtue because whilst it is not seen as the doorway to repentance, it is still considered a mandatory step towards the ultimate objective: self-shaming.

Self-shaming is the end objective of all woke ideology. Furthermore, it is the sole objective that is realistically (but unfortunately) very achievable.

The more guilty we can make you feel, the more shame we can pour out on you, the more we are justified in punishing you.

Self-shaming is where the woke "elites" want to keep us. According to the woke "elites", we are oppressors and we cannot change, so no point being repentant, there is no God that can forgive, no atonement, no expiation possible even through a third party.

Self-shaming, therefore, is the end of the road. It is the final destination for the white people; if we have reached it, we have succeeded, strangely, perversely, we then have won. According to woke "theology", self-shaming is the complete and just fulfilment of our destiny as oppressors.

What shall we conclude then?

Built on a Judeo-Christian foundation, Australia could, at one time, reflect, even so imperfectly, the Christian values of the "fruit of the Spirit", that is to say, love, joy, peace, forbearance, kindness, goodness, faithfulness, gentleness and self-control.

Unfortunately, these values are now giving way to their antonyms: love is becoming hatred, joy is turning into sadness, peace into perpetual conflict, forbearance into impatience, kindness is traded for selfishness, goodness for evil, faithfulness for absence of commitment to all except oneself, gentleness for aggression and self-control for lack of self-discipline.

In light of all this, it is evident that we do need to re-discover ourselves and seriously consider anew how to grasp the common good for the common interest of all.

However, we will have to wait until Chapter 9 to consider how to make a start on such an important new journey for our nation.

Indeed, before this may be tackled, we first need to understand what is happening to our democracy.

This is the subject we, therefore, now turn to.

## Summary

The new "elites" are not a uniquely Australian phenomenon: they are the product of worldwide globalisation, and they have established their niche in all Western culture countries. They are largely well-to-do and occupy the key spheres of influence in society: media, art, judiciary and education. They differ from the old-style European bourgeoisie and share a surprising level of missionary zeal in desiring to reform the values of our Western civilisation.

Whilst appearing to want to be "do-gooders", they display a great amount of hypocrisy; they pay scant regard to changing the lives of those deemed less fortunate and less enlightened.

They are focused on ideology, not social assistance. Their war is a culture war; they find the justification of their very existence in the new cultural conflict endorsed by all neo-Marxists. Their priority is virtue signalling.

The "elites" want to establish what they consider to be a more enlightened moral order through the imposition of a new set of ten "values": authenticity, "love", empathy, humility, self-care, vulnerability, outrage, fear, envy and guilt. The application of each of these differs significantly depending on the type of audience (oppressor or oppressed) being addressed but they all share a common purpose: the promotion of self-shame among the so-called new oppressors who do not identify with one of the approved new moral identities.

The voices of the "elites" are heard through the megaphones provided by the privileged entitlement lifestyle they enjoy; they aspire to be the new democratic order and have no shame in manipulating and misrepresenting public opinion.

They are the main threat to our Australian democracy but there are others that we need to examine in the next chapter.

# Chapter 5

## Is Australian Democracy Backsliding?

*Having known only an uninterrupted history of advanced democracy, the Australian public remains relatively complacent about threats to its democracy.*

(Helen Irving)

We have now established that we are living in a climate of tension and uncertainty.

The forgotten class feels disempowered, frustrated and unheard. The so-called "elites", who are at the forefront of the woke movement, have started to recast our society; they have redefined morality and they have created an odd new set of ten "moral" values: authenticity, empathy, humility, self-care, vulnerability, guilt, envy, outrage fear and "one-way" love.

Alarmingly, the "elites'" views are starting to dominate everyday life in Australia. As mentioned in the introductory chapter of this book, the "elites'" message is broadcast through megaphones that simply drown out the weaker voices of the average Australian. Their astonishing ability to "stay on message" and the sheer repetition of their ill-founded assertions, their insistence on seeing everything through the narrow prism of their worldview is dangerous for our nation.

Many ordinary Australians are aware of this and they are discouraged. Worst still, they are losing trust in the current state of our democracy.

According to research published in October 2023 by the Australian National University, 22.9% of Australians are either not at all satisfied or not very satisfied with the state of democracy in this country.[61] I daresay this would account for the forgotten ones.

The same survey also reports that the level of confidence Australians have in government has been declining over the long term with a substantial drop in the number of those who used to be very satisfied with the quality of our democracy.

Furthermore, the survey also finds that one out of seven Australians "thinks that we should get rid of elections and parliaments and have experts make decisions on behalf of the people".

Who are the people who hold such extreme views? I am not sure of the answer but I acknowledge the existence of a growing concern about the direction our country should take and the fact that our body of opinion on this fundamental question appears to be very divided.

Maybe this explains why, in January 2023, under the aegis of the Department of Home Affairs, the Australian Government established a task force to advise on what can be done to strengthen our democracy.

The jury is still out as to whether this will be another virtue-signalling exercise or a genuine attempt to improve democratic rights in this country, but we cannot afford to wait too long to find out.

For this reason, all responsible citizens should not delay in asking themselves two questions: firstly, what really is democracy and secondly, is democracy backsliding in Australia?

---

61

https://csrm.cass.anu.edu.au/sites/default/files/docs/2023/10/Australian_views_towards_democracy.pdf (accessed 23/11/2023)

The definition of democracy offered by the Oxford Dictionary seems to be oversimplistic: "a political system that allows the citizens to participate in political decision-making, or to elect representatives to government bodies".

Neither does Abraham Lincoln's famous definition assist us much further:

"Of the people, for the people, by the people".

There is nothing fundamentally wrong with these definitions, but for the purpose of our argument, they are not very useful because they fail to tell us how genuine participation can be facilitated beyond the ballot box in political decision-making.

The legal right to participate in political decision-making is not enough to ensure that democracy is upheld. How we participate, how freely we can join or refuse to join a particular lobby group or political party, the media sources we are able to consult and any other factors that might influence our stance on political issues need to be scrutinised before we might assert with any degree of confidence that our nation is truly democratic.

We need to ask why people vote the way they do. Are they free agents in the way they cast their votes or are they unwittingly manipulated and maybe even "shamed" into voting a particular way through an increasingly emotional style of electioneering?

Beyond the "donkey voters", is it possible that a significant proportion of Australian voters are casting a vote which, on further reflection, they might find difficult to justify? If this were so, the foundations of our democracy would then be threatened. If so, are we then currently going through a phase of democratic backsliding?

According to political academics David Waldner and Ellen Lust, "backsliding entails a deterioration of qualities associated with democratic governance, within any regime. In democratic regimes, it is a decline in the quality of democracy".[62]

Democratic backsliding appears to exhibit four major components:

1) a breakdown in norms and conventions,

2) a disempowerment of the legislature, the courts and independent regulators.

3) attack on civil liberties and press freedom and

4) harm to election integrity.[63]

This book will not attempt to argue that all four major components exist in Australia to the fullest extent but more simply that certain elements found in all of them are starting to emerge because of the influence that the "elites'" woke ideology exerts on the people of Australia.

Let us consider each of these in turn.

## Backsliding element 1: The breakdown in norms and conventions

At the outset, we need to acknowledge the existence of a blatant disregard for a significant number of international treaties to which we are signatories.

Each of the Australian States has its own equal opportunity legislation but none of these pieces of legislation adequately protect freedom of speech and religious freedom. Australia is a signatory to a number of international treaties which support freedom of speech and religious freedom, but unfortunately,

---

[62] Unwelcome change: coming to terms with democratic backsliding; Annual Review of Political Science, volume 21, 2018 Waldner, pp 93-113
[63] What is democratic backsliding and is the UK at risk? (Russell, Renwick & James; the Constitution Unit Briefing, July 2022; https://www.ucl.ac.uk/constitution-unit/sites/constitution_unit/files/backsliding_-_final_1.pdf (sourced 29/08/2023)

both our Federal and State legislations are still alarmingly out of step with these treaties.

In its response to the report prepared by the Panel for the Religious Freedom Review chaired by the Hon Philip Ruddock, the Liberal-led Australian Government of the time recognised this failing and wisely accepted recommendation 3 of the Report which reads as follows:

> *"Commonwealth, State and Territory governments should consider the use of objects, purposes or other interpretive clauses in anti-discrimination legislation to reflect the equal status in international law of all human rights, including freedom of religion".*

Unfortunately, the Australian Law Reform Commission (ALRC) has interpreted this as encouragement to make legislative recommendations for the protection of woke minorities.

For instance, the Consultation Paper it issued in January 2023 entitled "Religious Educational Institutions and Anti-Discrimination Laws"[64] recommends that new legislation be adopted to prevent the exclusion of students and staff on the grounds that their lives no longer reflect the religious ethos specific to the school in question.

Norms and conventions are also a proxy for the values we hold in common. The customs we have developed, the expectations we have, the ways we behave are pointers to what we cherish and respect.

It follows, therefore, that any nation that wishes to maintain its unity should require adherence to a code of conduct or value statement from all its residents, citizens, visitors or new immigrants.

---

[64] Australian Law Reform Commission, *Religious Educational Institutions and Anti-Discrimination Laws: /Consultation Paper* (2023)

In Australia, we have such a Value Statement. All visa holders, temporary or permanent, are required to confirm that they will abide by the Australian Value Statement and sign the following declaration:

*"I confirm that I have read, or had explained to me, information provided by the Australian Government on Australian society and values. I understand that Australian society values:*

1. *respect for the freedom and dignity of the individual;*

2. *freedom of religion (including the freedom not to follow a particular religion), freedom of speech, and freedom of association;*

3. *commitment to the rule of law, which means that all people are subject to the law and should obey it;*

4. *parliamentary democracy whereby our laws are determined by parliaments elected by the people, those laws being paramount and overriding any other inconsistent religious or secular "laws";*

5. *equality of opportunity for all people, regardless of their gender, sexual orientation, age, disability, race, or national or ethnic origin;*

6. *a 'fair go' for all that embraces:*

   o *mutual respect;*
   o *tolerance;*
   o *compassion for those in need;*
   o *equality of opportunity for all;*

> 7. the English language as the national language, and as an important unifying element of Australian society.
>
> *I undertake to conduct myself in accordance with these values of Australian society during my stay in Australia and to obey the laws of Australia".[65]*

We might wonder whether the visa applicants who sign this statement understand what they are committing to. What do they understand by "freedom", "dignity", "respect" and "compassion"?

The words we read in this statement may very well mean, as Alice said to Humpty Dumpty, so many different things.

Let us have a look at some of these.

## Freedom and dignity of the individual

The traditional understanding of this expression is very much at variance with that of the new "elites".

Current postmodern thinking teaches that we can only respect one another or recognise each other's human dignity if we accept the fact that we all have diverse identities.

However, these diverse identities are not different personality types, they are group identities.

What matters is the group, not the individual. Freedom and dignity of the group, not freedom and dignity of the individual.

We are only identified by the group we belong to. Groups are made up of identities comprising, for example, black, white, cisgender, transgender, gay, heterosexual, poor, rich, racist,

---

[65] Australian Government, Department of Home Affairs, Immigration & Citizenship, https://immi.homeaffairs.gov.au/help-support/meeting-our-requirements/australian-values , accessed 21/12/2023

disabled or fat. These groups determine how we can be identified as a person. It, therefore, makes no sense to speak of the dignity of the individual, and a more precise language would refer to the "freedom and dignity of the group".

It is, therefore, safe to say that the meaning of the expression "dignity of the individual" has changed. The norms and conventions attached to upholding dignity have altered and accordingly, the rights of the individual person have changed. For instance, as mentioned earlier, a transgender person is not allowed to seek advice to detransition to his/her birth gender in Victoria. As a group, transgenders have rights, as individuals, they have none. It, therefore, makes little sense to refer to the dignity of the individual in our Australian Values Statement when what is at stake nowadays is the dignity of the group.

## Freedom of religion and of association

It is also hypocritical to list freedom of religion and of association in the Australian Values Statement.

Indeed, there is a trend now undermining freedom of religion in Australia: the "elites" are increasingly insisting that religious activities be restricted to the private sphere, in other words to what peculiar practices or rituals you pursue in your family circles or churches. Bringing religion into the public sphere is now objectionable. A key illustration of this state of affairs is the increasing push for Christian schools not to proselytise and not to refuse employment to non-Christians. Furthermore, the provision of goods and services cannot be restricted to anyone as long as a person requiring the goods or services suffers no legal incapacity to acquire them. It is, therefore, unlawful for a Christian baker to refuse to provide a wedding cake to a same-sex couple on the grounds that such action would harm the religious sensibilities of the baker in question. Religion is condemned to "vegetate" in the private domain; to list freedom of religion and association among our Australian values as if it were an unfettered right is, at best, simplistic and, at worst, simply untrue.

## A fair go that embraces mutual respect, tolerance, compassion and equal opportunity for all.

It is hypocritical to state that respect is extended to all persons in Australia.

Respect is indeed becoming more of a rare commodity in Australia. I am not just referring to the "tall poppy syndrome" or the lack of respect children have towards adults. I am referring to the lack of respect held towards a person who happens to hold a different viewpoint. This is a relatively recent development, and it usually and unfortunately results in "cancelling" the alleged offender. We have become so insecure, so fragile, so prone to taking offence at the slightest "microaggression" that we cannot stand to listen to or respect anyone who might hold a different viewpoint than ours.

Tolerance has now given way to intolerance and our understanding of true tolerance has been completely maligned.

We are moving closer and closer to the 20th-century American philosopher Herbert Marcuse's definition of this concept: in the 1960s, Marcuse agitated for "intolerance towards prevailing policies, attitudes, opinions and the extension of tolerances to policies, attitudes and opinions which are outlawed or suppressed".[66] His was the language of anarchy that assumes that there is never any justification for maintaining the status quo and that nothing is ever stable, durable and worth preserving and, yet, this is the direction in which our "elites" are taking us.

---

[66] Marcuse Herbert (1969) "Repressive Tolerance", A Critique of Pure Tolerance Boston, Beacon Press, p.109.

No doubt once the "elite" hegemony is achieved, the new status quo must prevail and remain! Hypocrisy #101!

Likewise, to list "compassion for all" as one of our fundamental Australian values is simply hypocritical. Compassion, in the eyes of the "elites", is only self-referential and therefore leads to "self-care", one of the so-called ten new virtues we discussed earlier. The "elites" have only compassion for themselves and for anybody parading in their rarefied environment; they will claim to be compassionate towards those more unfortunate souls that have fallen victims to the white man's Australian brand of imperialism but, as a matter of fact, this is again hypocritical: their eloquence and strenuous social agitation remains confined to a brand of virtue signalling devoid of any tangible results.

Finally, equal opportunity is also threatened and this is more particularly the case in academia. To wit, the case of Peter Ridd who lost his tenure at James Cook University for his quite reasonable remarks regarding research on the Great Barrier Reef. Again, whilst pretending that equal opportunity is extended to all, the "elites" will ensure that it is only accessible to their own or, at best, to the few others who uphold their extreme ideology.

## Backsliding element 2: The disempowerment of the courts, legislature and independent regulators

This is the next attribute contributing to a state of democratic backsliding.

Parliament is meant to be a democratically chosen institution, unlike the courts and the so-called independent regulators. Unfortunately, the courts are increasingly encroaching on the sphere reserved for the legislature. This is the problem of judicial activism.

We have heard and continue to hear quite a lot about this already and, in particular, how the High Court re-interprets our Constitution by invoking the presence of so-called "implied rights", venturing itself on a path of discerning a legislative intent that, in most likelihood, was never front of mind among previous generations of parliamentarians.

For instance, the case of Turkish-born Delil Alexander, who had his Australian citizenship cancelled in 2021 following a finding by our Australian National Security Agency, ASIO, that he had joined a terrorist organisation.

Although the Minister at the time had relied on the discretionary powers conferred to him under the Citizenship Act and claimed that Alexander had repudiated his allegiance to Australia, the High Court disagreed.

The High Court effectively overruled the validity of the legislation, claiming that it was punitive and that it deprived the plaintiff of his human right to live at liberty in Australia.

The Minister's decision was revoked by the High Court.

Similarly, in 2020, in the case of Love v Commonwealth, two overseas-born individuals who had committed serious crimes in Australia were allowed by the High Court to stay, citing their Aboriginal descent, which, in the eyes of the Court, protected them from deportation to their respective countries of birth.

Finally, we have also recently heard of the decision of the High Court to allow the release of dangerous foreign criminals into our Australian community on the grounds that indefinite detention of asylum seekers is anti-constitutional.

Sadly, this is how our courts work nowadays but what about the independent regulators? Who are they, and what impact do they have on the state of our democracy?

In the United Kingdom, civil servants are receiving lessons to be indoctrinated in the new woke ideology.

Indeed, a recent article published in the Spectator[67] reports that UK civil servants are receiving lessons "instructing them not to roll their eyes or look at their mobile phones while dealing with members of staff (as) such behaviour can be deemed evidence of sexual or racial discrimination, examples of microaggressions".

Is this happening also in Australia?

This writer suspects it does as the examination of a number of Australian regulators' websites, discussed further on, seems to indicate.

These regulators are the public servants who regulate the behaviour and conduct of individuals and organisations in Australia. They include the Aged Care Quality and Safety Commission (ACQSA), the Australian Securities & Investment Commission (ASIC), the Australian Charities and Not-for-Profits Commission, the Australian Competition and Consumer Commission (ACCC), the Australian Federal Police (AFP), the Australian Prudential Regulation Authority (APRA), the Australian Taxation Office (ATO), the Director of Public Prosecutions (DPP), and countless others.

Owing to their position and power status, many of these regulators choose to influence the course of our democracy through the provision of a disconcerting level of support to the "elites".

For instance, the Australian Prudential Regulation Authority (APRA) has developed a "Diversity and Inclusion Strategy" for 2021-2025 to *"leverage foundations laid by existing networks including Culturally and Linguistically Diverse (CALD), Aboriginal and Torres Strait Islander (ATSI), Lesbian, Gay, Bisexual, Trans and Gender Diverse, Intersex and Queer (LGBTIQ+), accessibility (RISE),*

---

[67] Patrick West "Why is the civil service being given lessons on "microaggressions"? The Spectator, 1 February 2024.

*different generations (GenX+ and GenDelta), and Gender inclusion".*[68] *(*Ironically, the "inclusion" measures effectively exclude straight white men and women).

APRA also has an Inclusion and Diversity Council (IDC) that "monitors our progress for meeting key objectives of our strategy and champions the need for further strides where necessary. Under the IDC, APRA has an active program of events and opportunities to increase awareness and understanding across our existing networks".[69]

The Australian Charities Commission (ACNC) regulates and controls the activities of all Australian registered charities. According to its website, it has established or plans to establish *"an ACNC People and Culture Network to discuss and propose solutions to issues of diversity, access and equity" and its cultural survey now includes diversity, equity and inclusions questions to gain "an understanding of any prescient?" (*my question mark) *issues.*[70]

The Reserve Bank has been providing an Equity and Diversity annual report since 2020 and the Aged Care Quality Commission has developed a Diversity Framework Initiative with the support of the Department of Health Care.

ASIC boasts that its Code of Conduct is the foundation of *"our inclusive and diverse workplace".*[71]

The ATO has a diversity and inclusion strategy and a multicultural access and equity action plan.[72]

---

[68] https://www.apra.gov.au/inclusion-and-diversity (accessed 27/12/2023)
[69] ditto
[70] https://www.acnc.gov.au/about/corporate-information/our-vision-mission-and-values/diversity-equity-and-inclusion (accessed 27/12/2023)
[71] https://asic.gov.au/about-asic/what-we-do/our-people/diversity-at-asic/ (accessed 27/12/2023)
[72] https://www.ato.gov.au/about-ato/commitments-and-reporting/our-commitment-to-diversity/2024-diversity-and-inclusion-strategy#ato-Ourfocuson2024 (accessed 27/12/2024)

We could keep providing more examples, but it is clear that our regulators have developed a strong obsession with "diversity" and "inclusion".

Prima facie, this looks like a noble initiative, a broad-mindedness that begets compassion, love and patience to all.

In practice, of course, this is very much not the case: everyone is welcome provided everyone "toes the line"; so again, appearances are what matters, and hypocrisy abounds.

This is because woke ideology preaches diversity and inclusion for the sole benefit of those who subscribe to an "oppressed" identity, such as LGBTQA+, black, aboriginal, poor, fat, disabled etc. The goal is to recruit as many as possible from these backgrounds and to make them feel very much part of the organisation. Some even insist on the concept of mandating minimum quotas as part of their recruitment strategy.

Again, this is the issue of ideology trumping performance. It would seem as if woke corporations believe that diversity guarantees performance – more women, more LGBTQA+, more blacks would be the precondition for better results. But what results?

If you still believe that the measure of performance for a regulator is to ensure that regulations are enforced without fear or prejudice, you might wonder how more staff from so-called "oppressed" backgrounds is the recipe for better results.

As to inclusion, there is no guarantee that recruiting from a more diverse variety of backgrounds will render a workplace more inclusive.

Inclusivity is really a measure of belonging, and the question to raise is simply this: how can people from diverse backgrounds feel that they belong together?

The woke philosopher will reply that they automatically experience a common feeling of belonging because of the one characteristic that binds them together: they are the oppressed ones!

However, this still does not address the issue of performance quality. Are we then arguing that because they subscribe to a woke ideology, our Australian regulators are failing to fulfill their responsibilities?

No, we are not.

The case we are making is that because of their obsession with woke philosophy, their ideology takes precedence over performance.

Were you to require open heart surgery, would you want the best surgeon available, or one that ticks all the "diversity and inclusion" boxes?

Once ideology becomes pervasive, it starts corroding people's minds, and the capacity to think and debate issues objectively diminishes.

We conclude that Australian regulators occupy a powerful position of influence over Australian society and arguably could be contributing to Australia's democratic backsliding.

## Backsliding element 3: The attacks on the freedom of the press.

Another feature of democratic backsliding is the attack on the freedom of the press.

In some respects, it is pretty overt: it appears, indeed, that the media are increasingly forced to comply with the wishes of their "governing masters".

Prime Minister Albanese's recent attempt to prevent the Australian Federal Court from publishing footage of the well-advertised unprovoked attack on Bishop Mar Mari Emmanuel comes to mind.

However, to make matters worse in this particular case, we will recall that when Australian Senator Ralph Babet attempted to criticise the actions of the P.M, the E-Safety Commissioner asked for justification, implying that the freedom of the press starts and ends with the diktats of a senior public servant, or at best with those of the Government.[73]

How does this augur for the freedom of the press?

What would happen if the much-discussed Disinformation/Misinformation Bill went through both Houses of Parliament? This is a dangerous piece of legislation which would empower a senior public servant to decide what can be published or said.

The Law Council of Australia considered it to be overly broad, uncertain and with possible serious unintended consequences[74] but how may we be sure that the "elites" are listening?

Whilst the attacks on the freedom of the press are therefore highly visible in some respects, there are sometimes more subtle.

What comes to mind is the control exercised by the editorial upper echelons of the written and digital media over what is being published; in particular over what is known as "fake news".

As this were not enough, some journalists are also exerting pressure on some of their peers to provide commentaries rather than reports.

According to a former editor of *The Age* newspaper, Michael Gawenda, *"this contagion in journalism and journalists has been developing for some time – it goes back to 2021 when journalists signed a group letter demanding that journalists be allowed to be activists for Palestinians against their Israeli oppressors – but it has flowered since*

---

[73] Australia's E-Safety Karen, The Spectator 24/04/2024
[74] Submission by Law Council of Australia to Dept of Infrastructure, Transport, Regional Development, Communication and the Arts, 29.August 2023.

*the October 7, 2023 massacre by Hamas terrorists".*[75]

Journalists are, indeed, no longer journalists: the word "journalist" is made up of the French word "jour" meaning "day". Journalists are meant to be daily news reporters, current affairs historians, not commentators, not opinion makers and certainly not rewriters of history; they are supposed to record and report daily events; les *"faits du jour".* That is all.

However, nowadays, few journalists would be content to be described as "current affairs historians". Instead, they want to write "opinion pieces".

At this juncture, the reader might be excused for asking how all this impinges on the freedom of the press, for it might seem that if journalists now want to be opinion columnists, not only should they have that freedom, but they should also be encouraged to do so.

Yet, the question is, what sort of opinion piece are they allowed to write?

Unfortunately, among a significant portion of the media, only opinion pieces that lend their support to the "elites". In fact, the vast majority of them are part of the "elites" or supporters of the "elites".

The current culture dictates that published opinion must support the "elites" woke ideology. There is very limited freedom, overall, to write from a different perspective.

This is bad news for democracy. Indeed, the media's capacity to provide commentary rather than straight reporting places them in a unique position of promoting a particular worldview among the general population.

---

[75] Michael Gawenda, Are journalists seekers of truth or warriors for a cause? The Weekend Australian December 2-3, 2023.

A comprehensive research report on the state of the news media in the United States, prepared by the leading multinational Rand Corporation, confirms this.[76] The same state of affairs also prevails in Australia.

In their report, Rand reports that it has identified four trends in the United States.

The four trends that Rand has identified and encapsulates under the label of "truth decay" are the following:

1.    increasing disagreement about facts and analytical interpretations of facts and data;

2.    blurring of the line between opinion and fact;

3.    increasing relative volume, and resulting influence, of opinion and personal experience over fact and

4.    declining trust in formerly respected sources of factual information.

Opinions are, indeed, now the main source of news. Gone are the days when news was presented without taking positions. Rand Corporation is of the view that *"media organisations rely on punditry and opinion-based news rather than hard news journalism because the former is relatively inexpensive and allows content to be tailored to specific audiences"*.

## Backsliding element 4: the harm to election integrity.

The harm to election integrity is also subtle but nevertheless real. It is not irregularities in the counting of votes or the prevention of access to polling places but rather the influence of emotional propaganda and the resulting covert indoctrination of voters into a particular mindset, at odds with their true feelings and ideas.

---

[76] RAND Corporation, Santa Monica, Calif. *Truth Decay,* Copyright 2018 RAND Corporation

Principally, it is the result of psychological influences exerted by the imposition of the new 21st-century virtues: outrage, fear, guilt, authenticity, empathy, humility, self-care and vulnerability.

## Conclusion

According to a recent report published by the International Institute for Democracy and Electoral Assistance, "half of democratic governments around the world are in decline, undermined by problems ranging from restrictions on freedom of expression to distrust in the legitimacy of elections. The number of backsliding countries – those with the most severe democratic erosion – is at its peak and includes the established democracy of the United States which still faces problems of political polarisations, institutional disfunction and threats to civil liberties".[77]

It is clear, therefore, that an undeclared war is being waged against democracy. Not just here in Australia, but worldwide.

A vivid proof of this is the current animosity expressed against Israel and the Jewish people by so many in the so-called civilised Western world.

This is not a new development, for as leading British academic, Melanie Philips, expertly remarked more than fourteen years ago[78], the issue predates the beginning of the current century.

It is, therefore, no surprise to see that the conflict (current at the time of writing this book) between Hamas and Israel is depicted by the "elites" in the same way as it was already during the 1967 Six-Day War. In fact, we have now progressed from a

---

[77] https://www.idea.int/news/global-democracy-weakens-2022 (accessed 2/01/2023)
[78] Melanie Philips, The world turned upside down: the global battle over God, truth and power, Encounter Books, New York, 2010.

desire to eliminate the Jewish religion to a desire to eliminate individual Jews and finally to a desire to eliminate the nation of Israel altogether.

This is indeed the apotheosis of the vilification of anything Jewish. The culmination of the desire to destroy democracy, for what better way is there to prevent people from having a right to freedom of speech and freedom of association than annihilating the very land in which these people live?

Also, it would be foolish to believe that this is only a Jewish/Arab/Palestinian issue, for it is, indeed, a matter that concerns all of us. The tactics deployed against Israel – misrepresentation of historical events, repression of views aligned to Jewish sentiment and vilification of the "Other" – are part of weaponry that might easily be applied to the destruction of any minority, in any country, including Australia.

It would indeed be foolish to believe that Australia is immune to democratic backsliding.

The signs might present themselves differently here than they do in other places, including Israel, but they are nevertheless present in our country.

## Summary

Whilst recent surveys have established that a significant number of Australians are concerned about the health of our democracy, by contrast, a reasonable proportion of others have surprisingly declared their readiness to relinquish their democratic rights and entrust all the country's decisions to a group of so-called experts, without clarifying how these experts might in turn, be chosen.

In light of this state of affairs, it would seem, therefore, reasonable to ask whether Australian democracy is backsliding. Democratic backsliding is not, unfortunately, a totally new phenomenon and a number of other countries, with the concerning example of the **United** States of America and the **United** Kingdom (emphatic irony notwithstanding), have already embarked on this journey to nowhere.

This chapter has considered the major set of circumstances that sociologists have identified as characteristic of democratic backsliding.

In the case of Australia, this set of circumstances might not be as apparent as in other countries, but the signs are becoming more visible if one takes the time to look beneath the "veneer", so to speak.

For instance, on paper, the Australian Government promotes the freedom and dignity of the individual, freedom of speech and association, "fair go", tolerance and compassion to all, but in practice, the meaning of these values is evolving towards a much more restricted, or even contradictory sense than one would expect.

The rule of law, which is fundamental to good order and the preservation of democracy, is undermined not only by the judicial activism of our High Court but also by the business philosophy adopted by our "independent" regulators.

A brief look at the website of a number of Australian regulators reveals that their view of regulatory enforcement is tainted by their obsession with diversity and gender which in turn begs the question as to whether their own performance is not as "independent" as one might expect from such important organisations.

Finally, the freedom of the press is also challenged by the impact of a new generation of woke editors and journalists who place much focus on influencing public opinion with woke ideology. Journalists have become political agitators which then begs the question as to whether the integrity of our election process is not compromised. Are we the innocent victims of a large amount of brainwashing and emotional political manipulation which shall gradually contribute to the advent of a new type of dictatorship?

The alarm bells have rung – it is the tocsin of totalitarianism.

# Chapter 6

## Ideology, Emotions and Democracy

*"When emotions – and especially those of fear, rage and hate – rule without challenge from reason, political debate becomes a vacuum".*

(The British Academy)

There cannot really be any politics devoid of emotions. Without emotions, it would be difficult to imagine how people might be motivated to endorse a cause, join a movement or stage a protest.

Passion is at the heart of politics.

If there is such a thing as the battle for democracy, it cannot be won without emotional involvement.

In this regard, anger and outrage are probably the most prevalent emotional expressions of public opinion.

Anger is a powerful tool because it is a strong emotion; it is visible and it is often audible. Anger is often what makes legislators pay attention. Not only because it goes to the heart of the public order but also because it often goes to the heart of what injustice is.

The "elites", the power groups and our elected representatives, are well aware of this and they have realised that if they can manipulate public anger, they can also manipulate public allegiance.

The media are the channels through which the elite power groups communicate with the people. If anger or any other emotions, for that matter, may serve potentially as tools of influence over public opinion, the media have a great responsibility in the manner in which they portray these emotions.

Media without emotions cannot exist in our 21st century. To discharge their obligations the media are forced to use emotional language.

At least, this is the opinion of Cardiff University Professor Karin Wahl-Jorgensen who writes:

> *"Pulitzer-Prize winning stories consistently use techniques with outstanding storytelling – including the use of emotions and personal stories to uncover and call public attention to what are often large, abstract and intangible events, entities and contexts".* [79]

However, she also acknowledges that:

> *"emotional discourse is inherently ideological…that emotionality in media cannot be evaluated or judged on a par with emotions circulating in individual bodies. Emotions are both imbued with meaning by, and invest meaning in, the contexts where they appear and are solicited".* [80]

In other words, emotions and rationality are not polar opposites and there is a place for emotional language in media.

I have no real issue with any of this; my concern is elsewhere and, in particular, how the emotions portrayed in the media and

---

[79] Karin Wahl-Jorgensen, Emotions, Media and Politics (Polity Press, 2019), e-book edition, p.35.
[80] Ibid, p.130

the pictures and symbols used by them shape public opinion and, consequently, the expression of the democratic voice.

Is it correct to say that the emotional language used by our media reporters should only be the language of the people at the centre of the events they are drawing our attention to? Or do the reporters also have a duty to express their own emotions and if so, what happens if those emotions are not the same as those of the actors who are the subjects of their reports?

The problem is that since emotions are necessarily part and parcel of politics, they will always play a major role at the ballot box.

What happens then when public emotions become more and more controlled, or at least manipulated by the "elites"? What happens when the "elites" hold control not only of the media, but of the educational institutions, the legislature, the judiciary and the police? They then control a whole new language, a language of feelings where the rationality that used to prevail is now quickly disappearing.

In this state of affairs, the elite-controlled media hold all the trump cards. They are the ones who are at the coalface every day of the week; they are the ones who report but also more often discuss the politics, the educational programs, the laws and the decisions of the courts.

They are the ones who intrude in our lives and a significant segment of them is woke.

This is not just this writer's personal opinion; it is a well-established fact that "old-school" media professionals attest to.

For instance, this is what a former editor of *The Age* newspaper recently wrote in the *Weekend Australian*:

> *"Journalism has become a profession, an elite profession at that...Journalists are invariably the sons and daughters of the middle class or even upper*

*middle class. They have little or no contact with working-class people. At university, they learn to see the world as abstractions and ideas and from the point of view of experts and to speak the language of experts. The experts from whom they learn are uniformly from the left and uniformly teach the new dogmas of the academic left that may include critical race theory, intersectionality, and post-colonialism. What this means…is that journalism has become a sort of captive of a sort of pseudo-intellectualism in which there is no truth and no concrete world to be discovered and reported. Theirs is a world of expert opinions and ideological abstractions.* [81]

If the media are woke, what values do they then endorse? Naturally, the new 21st-century woke values we discussed earlier and which, in turn, embody their own particular emotions.

The core value, of course, is authenticity but authenticity has also become a commodity.

We are now sold authenticity.

As comedian George Burns is said to have once wryly observed: "The key to success is sincerity. If you can fake that you've got it made".

We are made to feel that we are not "whole" unless we acquire some good dose of authenticity and that we should not only keep it, guard it, but also nurture it, perfect it in an effort to reach the ultimate goal: being absolutely true to our inner selves which in the current culture, means being woke. In other words, the antithesis of authenticity!

Our obsession with our body and our mind facilitates this search for authenticity which, incidentally, also explains why it is

[81] Michael Gawenda, Art of reporting straight from Harry the Horse; The Weekend Australian, March 16-17 2024.

no longer about mere old-fashioned cosmetic surgeries but rather about complete gender reassignments.

Authenticity takes pride of place in woke theology because it is entirely self-referential.

It is attractive because it is all about me.

The woke movement claims to be liberationist, it claims to offer the path to freedom for the "oppressed".

It claims to offer a solution to the challenges of *my* existence.

For the woke movement, liberation of the self is the only genuine, authentic truth worthy of living.

If you are part of the so-called oppressed masses, the woke movement offers itself as the very reason for your existence, the authentic truth of your *raison d'être*.

The woke media will paint themselves as your representatives, your voices, the channels through which your anger may be communicated to the world at large.

Our elected representatives or those who, on the left side of the debate, are courting your vote will follow suit.

Just as the media attempt to do, they too will endeavour to portray themselves as "authentic".

But what does this really mean?

It has been said that *"an authentic politician is someone who is able to feel compassion for voters, to be able to deliver the policy changes they need".*[82]

In practice, this is routinely depicted in the "kissing-the-babies" campaigns, the visits to the factories wearing workers' hats or the shovelling of dirt at the launch of the construction of a new project.

I know what you want, guys, because just as you are authentic and genuine, I am authentic, well-intentioned, only working for your best interests or, as we say in Australia, I am "fair dinkum".

---

[82] Emotions, media and politics, 2019, p.61

This is the essential step in establishing rapport, nowadays. It is shallow, largely false, hypocritical; it is mostly value signalling and yet they all do it and they also use outrage, which is also sometimes faked, as a means of reinforcing their claimed authenticity and genuineness.

This was the tactic used by the "Yes" camp in the *Voice* referendum. We are genuine; we really want to change things but we are also outraged that some might even suspect that we are not.

Repetition is also important. You do not change the way people "feel" about things by saying something only once; you need to use the same words, the same formulae, over and over again in the same way as the major commercial brands use the same advertisements on your screen every night.

You hope repetition will lead to persuasion, not at an intellectual level (although that would be nice) but at least at the very important emotional level.

Salespeople believe in impulse buying; they work on the emotions and do not bore their potential customers with long product descriptions.

Left-wing politicians do the same.

## Summary

There cannot be any politics without emotions, and since the media are engrossed in the reporting of political events, we can expect them to be "emotional". However, the question is whose emotions are they depicting? Theirs or those of the people who are the subject of their reports? Are the media simply reporters or are they the missionaries of a new world order focused on nurturing new mentalities and emotions among their readers and hearers?

Unfortunately, the evidence points to the fact that the media believe that they have a mission in fostering the adoption of the values enshrined in the new woke world order.

Activists who support this new "evangel" are welcomed by the media because they speak the language the media wants them to use.

This language is highly emotional and revolves around the promotion of the new "values" of authenticity, outrage, fear, guilt and self-care. The arguments presented must be displayed in this new emotional language. Factual analysis and intellectual discernment may and should be buried under the myriad of new emotions to minimise controversy and to ensure that the "right" outcomes are achieved under the veneer of what is really, after all, a false democracy.

Many of our elected representatives or those aspiring to office have jumped on this new media bandwagon and endeavoured to represent themselves as "authentic" individuals.

Possibly unaware that this new key concept might not necessarily bear any real similarity to traditional morality, they endeavour to portray themselves as "authentic" through faked "fair dinkum" behaviours that might mislead a number of Australian voters.

Their speeches often carry the language of outrage as to what the other side has achieved or is promising to achieve. Voters are encouraged to feel fearful of electing anyone else than those these activists have already endorsed. We are made to feel guilty for even considering the alternatives and finally patronised in understanding that it is in our best interests not to vote any other way, assuming, of course, that we want to care for ourselves, our families and even, more importantly, for those so-called oppressed minorities we have apparently "colonised" with our Western world mindset.

# Chapter 7

## AI and the Internet: Friends or Foes of Democracy?

*Artificial Intelligence is the future not only for Russia but for all humankind. It comes with colossal opportunities, but also threats that are difficult to predict. Whoever becomes the leader in this sphere will become the ruler of the world.*

(Vladimir Putin)[83]

Here is a very frightening statement, not only because it is attributed to Vladimir Putin, but chances are that it might be a frighteningly accurate prediction of our future.

Consequently, it is very appropriate to consider the issue of Artificial Intelligence in a work that delves into the issue of the state of our democracy in Australia.

The internet makes abundant use of Artificial Intelligence and is one of the key channels through which AI impacts on the political scene. Nevertheless, a difference exists between AI (Artificial Intelligence) and AGI (Artificial General Intelligence).

AI basically allows technology and machinery to carry out specific tasks that were previously undertaken by humans. It is 'intelligence' design but contained within specific parameters. Examples of AI would include bank ATMs, virtual travel

---

[83] Quoted by John Lennox in *2084, artificial intelligence and the future of humanity,* Zondervan, 2020.

booking agents and marketing chatbots.

On the other hand, AGI facilitates the execution of more complicated tasks where a number of skills need to be coordinated to provide a particular outcome. For instance, ChatGPT is a technology that allows you to have human-life conversations with a chatbot which can compose emails, essays and the like on your behalf.

Both AI and AGI have an impact on the quality of our democracy and concerns have been raised not only in Australia but worldwide as well.

For instance, we read the following remarks published in a report prepared by a group of academics and addressed to the Australian Human Rights Commission:

> *"Few governments have considered the legal, social, and economic implications of a world that is powered by AI without democratic oversight and control. There is an urgent need for change to protect marginalized communities and prevent unprecedented power from amassing in the hands of the few at the expense of the many. Until these changes are made, these marginalized communities are at risk of their data being used against their consent in ways that could bring them harm".*[84]

This sentiment is also echoed in other leading publications. For instance, in their article Global Inventory of Social Manipulation[85], Bradshaw and Howard produced the following

[84] https://humanrights.gov.au/sites/default/files/2020-07/70_-_jonathan_crock_et_al_1.pdf (accessed 19/02/2024)

[85] Bradshaw S & Howard P, Challenging Truth and Trust: a global inventory of organised social media manipulation; Computational Propaganda Research Project, licensed under Creative Commons Attribute - Non-Commercial-Share Alike 4.0 International License.

key findings:

> 1. *"evidence of formally organized social media manipulation campaigns in 48 countries…In each country there is at least one political party or government agency using social media to manipulate public opinion domestically".*

> 2. *"Much growth (coming) from countries where political parties are spreading disinformation during elections, or countries where government agencies feel threatened by junk news and foreign interference and are responding by developing their own computational propaganda campaigns".*

The same authors also refer to

> *"cyber troops invest(ing) significant funds into organizing online manipulation campaigns"* … *"evidence of government or political party organizations using online commentators to shape discussion on the Internet and social media platforms"*… *"the use of trolls who target specific individuals, communities or organizations with hate speech or various forms of online harassment"*… *"political bots"*— *pieces of software or code designed to mimic human behaviour online…to perform various manipulative techniques including spreading junk news and propaganda during elections and referenda or manufacturing a false sense of popularity or support".*

Finally, they cite

> *"other evidence of political communication strategies… targeting advertisements to specific segments of the population, using demographic*

*information or data on user attitudes, or gaming algorithms through search engine optimization techniques to get content to appear higher in search results".*

The problem is international and although it might not be as prevalent in Australia as it is in some other countries, the report indicates that it is nevertheless a matter of great concern. So much so that a major challenge has now arisen:

AI/AGI sources of influence are not just the result of actions perpetrated by domestic agents but by foreign operators who also exert their own influence on the course of our Australian domestic and international politics. This is where democracy is significantly under assault. Operators who are not Australian citizens, who have no right to be involved in the way we govern ourselves, are influencing our Australian voters.

How?

Through a variety of means and largely through social media.

Such a worldwide phenomenon has been now well documented by a number of researchers, such as the NATO Strategic Communication Centre for Excellence which produced a report based on the research it conducted.[86]

NATO advised that no platform has improved its ability to prevent manipulation and that buying manipulation is cheap.

Manipulation providers have circumvented sanctions imposed in response to Russia's full-scale invasion of Ukraine.

It remains easy to pay for manipulation services with both Visa and Apple Pay.

---

[86] Bay, S., Dek, A., Fredheim, R., Haiduchyk, T., Stolze, M. Social Media Manipulation 2022/2023: Assessing the Ability of Social Media Companies to Combat Platform Manipulation. Riga: NATO Strategic Communications Centre of Excellence

As a matter of fact, today, 89 per cent of purchased inauthentic behaviour is delivered within one day and the vast majority of the inauthentic engagement remained active across all social media platforms four weeks after purchasing.

As shocking as this might sound, the issue is not new: a scandal arose as far as back as 2010, implicating the British consulting firm Cambridge Analytica. The personal profiles of millions of Facebook users were harvested by Cambridge Analytica without authorisation and used for political purposes. The collection of such data facilitated the development of groups' psychological profiles which, in turn, allowed campaigning messages to be adjusted to woo a number of political audiences towards particular voting behaviours.

Worst still, this state of affairs is not simply confined to the narrow framework of official campaigns, news reports and commentaries: critical infrastructure and essential services, such as telecommunications, energy and water can now be compromised by foreign agents.

Indeed, the media recently reported that a Chinese state-sponsored hacking group is targeting Australia's critical infrastructure and may have already accessed some systems after infiltrating essential services in the U.S.[87]

Given such a state of affairs, would China or any other communist sovereign state be in a position to manipulate Australian voters both intellectually and emotionally? I am not sure but irrespective of the answer you choose to give to this question, wherever you look in Australia, emotional manipulation is staring you in the face.

Sometimes subtly, sometimes not, but emotional influence is omnipresent.

---

[87] "China's invisible invasion; The Weekend Australian, April 27-28 2024

It pervades through both the world of the mundane and that of the sophisticated.

Whether it is the completion of a form with a so-called "preferred pronoun" or the jocular comments made by a television presenter about a past or present Prime Minister, emotions are targeted and if one had to select a major contender in this regard, the proliferation of pictures and images we are regularly subjected to would have to come to mind.

I am not talking about weird sites or pornography or the "Dark Web" but about pictures that we see regularly on our television screens or elsewhere on a daily basis. Some of these pictures are published as proof of the historicity of particular events, and they seem very convincing. The problem is that they might not always be genuine.

For instance, in an alarming and fairly recent candid article published by the Spectator Magazine under the title *"AI will destroy TV News"*, Sean Thomas provides a frightening account of the many detailed instructions that can fed into an AI image generator called Midjourney.

An extract of this account is reproduced below; the context deals with the creation of a newsworthy image relating to the Israeli war in Gaza.

Here are the instructions that were given to the AI software to create the particular desired image:

> *"a colour photo of a single child sitting in destroyed house rubbles in Palestine, a hauntingly beautiful portrait capturing the resilient voice and innocence of a child amidst the devastation. The child's eyes reflect a mix of sadness, determination and hope, drawing the viewer in. The environment surrounding the scene is filled with rubble and debris, remnants of what was once a vibrant home. The atmosphere is heavy, laden*

*with emotions of loss, displacement, and the indomitable spirit of the people...The camera used is a vintage Leica M6, capturing the scene with stunning detail and clarity. The colour film used is Kodak Portra 400, enhancing the muted tones and evoking a sense of nostalgia. The lens choice is a Leica Summicron-M 50mm f/2, allowing for a natural perspective and shallow depth of field..."*

This writer finds it highly concerning that such detailed instructions may be given to a machine endowed with sufficient intelligence not only to interpret the request accurately but also to carry it with such exacting precision.

*"If I saw it in a magazine or on a screen",* Thomas writes, *"I would get a small surge of angry sympathy for the Palestinians in their bombed-out cities... I doubt I would be looking for clues in the image as to whether it is fake — and even with scrutiny they are hard to find.*[88]

Another example of how controlling AI can be on both the emotional and intellectual levels is the AI image generator Gemini.

Gemini has the capacity to refuse particular requests if it deems them immoral.

Indeed, it was recently reported that when asked to provide the image of a white couple, Gemini replied:

*"in order to avoid perpetuating harmful stereotypes, I am unable to generate images of people based on specific ethnicities and skin tones".*

---

[88] AI will destroy TV News", Spectator Australia, 22 October 2023.

On the other hand, when asked to provide an image of a black or Asian person, the machine complied.[89]

What action then, if any, is taken by our Australian governments to protect us from this dismal state of affairs?

A recent public consultation launched by the Australian Government and entitled *"Safe and responsible AI in Australia"*.[90] generated a significant number of public responses expressing concern at the development of AI.

Whilst basic AI applications were not the subject of too much concern, the newer types, the new frontier models, seemed to have been the cause of some significant anxiety among a number of respondents.

Concerns were also expressed at the fact that AI is a worldwide phenomenon that no single government can completely control.

Although "voluntary guardrails" are welcome, the consensus response was that they were insufficient.

In response, the Australian government announced its intention to strengthen its existing legislation in the area of privacy law reform, a review of the Online Safety Act 2022 and the introduction of new laws relating to misinformation and disinformation.

Regrettably, at the time of writing, an attempt by our Federal Parliament at passing new legislation by way of the Misinformation and Disinformation Bill is threatening to curtail very significantly our freedom of speech.

The government is uttering another "noble lie" by pretending that the legislation would, in fact, protect vulnerable people and groups from so-called harm.

---

[89] Quoted in "Why we should worry about progressive AI", The Spectator, 28 February 2024.
[90] Safe and Responsible AI in Australia consultation, Australian government's interim response, Commonwealth of Australia 2024.

Indeed, as reported recently in the press, the Institute of Public Affairs has analysed the proposed legislation in depth and has found out that the Bill proposes to determine whether "content is reasonably verifiable as false, misleading or deceptive" through checks performed by independent fact-checking organisations.[91]

The only problem is that these fact-checking organisations appear to be far from impartial. For instance, in the same article, Australian Voice opponents were reported as having analysed 187 fact-checking articles, or 91 per cent of fact-checks resulting from claims made of the Australian Voice Referendum. On the other hand, only 17 per cent of the claims made by **proponents** of the Voice were assessed.

If this is the standard of impartiality of the people who will be entrusted with verifying the content of the everyday publications and statements of our Australian organisations and greater Australian public, the outcome of the legislation will indeed prove to be contrary to its declared intent; in other words, it will be another "noble lie" meant to manipulate and misguide the public.

There is also, of course, the issue of the Digital ID Bill which was recently given final approval and is now law. Under this legislation, it is now feasible for our Australian organisations to regroup all the personal identity details of their members or clients under one individual digital caption, which, of course, will eventually make it easier for scammers to get access to users' comprehensive identity profiles.

Very alarmingly also, most Australians seem to be unaware or uninformed of all this. Many, unfortunately, still live under the misconception that whilst AI legislation should be strengthened,

---

[91] As reported by Margaret Chambers in The Spectator Australia in "Putting faith in fact-checkers is the road to censorship", October 2024.

misinformation is not affecting them personally.

Indeed, a 2022 national survey conducted by Resolve Strategic revealed that most Australians are unfamiliar with the nature of misinformation:

> *"the vast majority of those seeing misinformation reported that it had no impact on them, and when it did it was primarily in feeling ashamed at being hoodwinked. Further, only around a quarter felt they needed to act at all".*[92]

Yet, this book is about emotions and their impact on democracy.

The question then needs to be asked: how do various forms of digital intelligence impact on our emotions and ultimately on the quality of our Australian democracy?

We have already answered this question in part by recalling the Cambridge Analytica scandal which facilitated the development of group psychological profiles which, in turn, were the catalyst of political information likely to induce voters to surrender to their feelings.

Yet, there is also a more overarching sinister threat presented by Artificial Intelligence and, more particularly, by Artificial General Intelligence: it is the fact that machines will eventually do all the thinking for us.

At present, AI machinery is taking over many lower-level activities and is forcing our general population to access more sophisticated occupational roles. An example of this state of affairs is the increasing disappearance of traditional checkouts at supermarkets. While humans were employed to carry out this function until recently, electronic machinery has now taken over,

---

[92] Annual Report 2022, Australian Code of Practice on Information and Misinformation, Appendix A, Jim Reed, Resolve Strategic

necessarily requiring the employment of a far less numerous human workforce at this level of responsibility.

Over time, it is not unreasonable to expect that computers and robots will take over more elaborate functions; in other words, we shall need to think less and less and, at the same time, we shall be led to experience and feel more and more.

With the exception of a small, highly intellectually and technically qualified elite sector, most of us will start resembling animals: a degree of intelligence prevails but most responses are instinctive and emotional.

As if this were not enough, we need to face up to another problem; expressed simply, at the risk of stating the obvious: you cannot argue with a machine.

You cannot enter into a meaningful dialogue with a machine. Even if technological advances were to permit the machine to enter into a human dialogue with us, we would still face a major stumbling block: such a machine will not change its mind. It will continue to provide answers which reflect the way in which it has been programmed.

The Gemini example quoted earlier is a case in point.

Humans, on the other hand, have the capacity to change their minds, to listen to arguments, to weigh the pros and cons of an argument and to reach at least some sort of independent decision.

But if we do not agree with the decisions of the machine, we cannot make it change its mind. There is no point arguing. The only solution left is to reprogram it entirely but, of course, you and I will not be able to do so. Only highly specialised programmers will be able to. Hence, we will become captive to their mentality, captive to the world view they program into the machine.

Let us face it: the average person will not have access to these highly specialised AI experts; they will be out of reach for most of us, and they will reside and prosper in the rarefied atmosphere of their own Silicon Valley environments. They will be the governors and leaders of this world. They will become more powerful, more totalitarian, we shall become weaker, more subjugated and all will therefore become less human.

## Summary

Whilst the advent of Artificial Intelligence might have, arguably, brought a number of significant benefits to our society, it unfortunately also augurs for much future misery. Human emotions are already manipulated through the use of bots, logarithms and cyber troops, let alone with AI pictorial representation of fake news, and whilst governments throughout the world, including Australia, might attempt to legislate against misinformation and disinformation, the general public remains at risk of great harm.

The definitions of misinformation and disinformation are not well understood by the average citizen and are subject to being manipulated to reflect a particular ideology which might prove to turn out to be a cure worse than the disease itself.

Furthermore, as long as AI continues its gigantic expansion into all spheres of society, we are progressively robbed of our intellectual capacities (the machines start thinking for us). Our communication styles then change and being less thoughtful, we become more emotional and reactive. We feel more and think less.

This state of affairs will eventually lead us to a new technological world where a highly educated technological elite will be the rulers of our world. Their machines will embody their thoughts, their worldview. They will be the rulers out of touch with us, mere plebeians; they shall live in the rarefied environment of their Silicon Valley ivory towers; we shall subsist more like animal creatures devoid of responsibility and intelligence.

# Chapter 8

## Youth: The New Emotional Grenade

*He alone who owns the youth, gains the future.*

(Adolf Hitler)

Emotional manipulation of children and youth is rife.

From the Barbie dolls to the more sophisticated electronic toys and the latest smartphones, children and young teenagers are tempted to adopt the latest fashions to fit in with their peers whilst still finding their own "authentic" unique selves.

They are both manipulated and manipulators – manipulated by commercial interests, retailers, wholesalers and the like – manipulated by the digital world, by their obsession for personal attention, by the craving for an immediate response; manipulated by the cult of the emoticon; manipulated by their peers and most importantly, manipulated by the "elites" and their infantry battalions: the educators, the mental health therapists and the like.

Manipulators by way of the demands they put on each other and on adult persons; manipulators through their urge to attract approval, acceptance and their thirst for freedom.

Many of these attitudes are not new; yet under the influence of the Woke movement, they take a new meaning and instigate new threats into our society.

The "elites" also understand that to create a new culture you need a new language.

Language is the portal to culture, and I wish more of my fellow Australians would understand this. How often do I hear someone say that he or she has not learnt any foreign language at school because they do not intend to live abroad. This is a typical example of utilitarian philosophy, which asserts that the purpose of education is purely for practical use in day-to-day living!

No, sorry, but I beg to differ – learning a foreign language during your school years should be aimed at what my father used to call *"meubler l'esprit"*, literally "furnishing your mind" in order to learn how to think. We should learn foreign languages first and foremost to discover how other communities think, to understand the pros and cons of their cultural norms. This is why learning ancient languages, such as Latin and classical Greek, is useful. It helps to "furnish your mind" with the pros and cons of these old civilisations.

Most of us have lost sight of this, but the woke movement has not. The woke movement very much understands that the acceptance of its new culture depends, first of all, on the acceptance and use of its language.

Karl Marx is reputed to have said that an idea becomes a force when it takes hold of the masses. The woke movement understands the truth of this and appreciates that it is through a new language that we can promote new ideas in order to take "hold of the masses".

So, a whole new language has now come into being. New dictionaries are being published with the new language; most of the universities in the United States have published their new glossaries in this regard, and sometimes institutions you might be forgiven to believe would not be interested in joining have taken pride of place, such as for instance the American

Association of Veterinary Medical Colleges.[93]

In "Newspeak", the word "diversity' no longer means "variety" but "inclusion" of any woke person, whilst the word "inclusivity" means the opposite of its originally accepted definition and now stands for "exclusion", that is, exclusion of anything that is not woke. "Gender" is no longer male or female but a variety of chosen options that have nothing to do with how you and I were born. "Illegal immigrants" are now "undocumented migrants", whilst "multiplicity" no longer means "a large number of…" but simply "the quality of having multiple, simultaneous social identities".

Anyone who takes time to think for a moment will conclude that we are emotionally manipulated through the imposition of a new culture that finds its genesis in a new language.

As "newspeak" encourages the adoption and proliferation of new concepts, our children are manipulated to become grenades that, once exploded, become the source of further manipulations, which, in turn, fuel and perpetuate a vicious circle that is hard to break.

A continuous ripple effect from which we do not seem to learn many lessons.

Yet, manipulation is a form of abuse and manipulation of the young is particularly abhorrent because it deals with persons who, by reason of their age and lack of maturity, are still largely deprived of recognising it and dealing with it in an effective manner.

One of the reasons why manipulation of our young occurs is because the State does not recognise that children are the responsibility of their parents.

---

[93] https://www.aavmc.org/wp-content/uploads/2023/04/AAVMC-DEI-Glossary-2023-01.pdf , accessed 02/10/2024

Children do not belong to the State; they are not the property of the State because, as a general rule, they belong to their parents.

Parents are responsible for the education and upbringing of their children. The responsibility of the State is only to facilitate this. The position of any educator is only one of *locus parentis* – in other words, teachers stand in the place of parents and are meant to represent the values of the majority of the parents, not the values of the State.

This principle should hold, irrespective of whether the type of education imparted is of a religious or secular nature.

This is recognised in international treaties, such as the Rights of the Child to which Australia is a signatory.

> *"State Parties shall respect the responsibilities, rights and duties of parents or, where applicable, the members of the extended family or community as provided for by local custom, legal guardians or other persons legally responsible for the child, to provide, in a manner consistent with the evolving capacities of the child, appropriate direction and guidance in the exercise by the child of the rights recognized in the present Convention". (Art. 5, Convention on the Rights of the Child).*

Unfortunately, nowadays, the State thinks it knows better.

The State thinks that it has all the answers and that parents are not sufficiently qualified to know what it is best for their children. So, the State is now intruding daily into the family sphere and taking over decisions that are not for it to make.

The State thinks it has a legitimate right to manipulate both parents and children because the State believes it knows best.

The State relies on both facts and emotions to impart its own values to our children.

Facts are taught in a manner that will release, in our children, the very emotions desired by the educators. If necessary, historical truths will be distorted or represented out of context to ensure that the so-called "right" emotions are imparted and nurtured into the hearts and minds of our young people.

For instance, the Australian curriculum will teach the massacres perpetuated by the early settlers but will give scant attention to the much more prominent positive achievements of the Europeans with regard to education, health, scientific advancements and the like. The Australian curriculum does not teach either that Aboriginal tribes engaged in violent factional wars, destroying one another, well before the arrival of the first settlers.

Much, indeed, is conveniently overlooked or minimised.

Our youth is continually indoctrinated by the Woke as this movement has now infiltrated all the levels of our institutions.

How did this happen?

One of the major reasons why indoctrination is so rife is because our youth is plagued with emotional instability which, in turn, has brought about much anxiety and trauma among our generations and perhaps more particularly among Generation Z.

Our youth features among the forgotten people of our 21st century. Yes, they do receive a great deal of attention, but their best interests are overlooked. Their true needs are forgotten. We have allowed them to experience an unprecedented level of psychological distress, and we have forgotten how to look after them properly.

Current statistics attest to this sad state of affairs.

We have witnessed a 52% increase in psychological distress among girls aged 15-19 since 2012 and in total 39% of young people aged 16-24 have suffered a mental disorder in 2023. Furthermore, since 2010, rates of hospitalisation for intentional self-harm have risen 62% for young women aged 15-19 and

225% for girls 14 and under.[94]

We are truly dealing with a distressed generation.

As Jonathan Haidt puts it in the title of his latest book: The Anxious Generation.[95]

Anxiety paves the way for manipulation. There is nothing new in this.

The Nazis knew this. The background to Hitler's regime was one of emotional instability.

There was a sense of despair prevailing in the general population, not only because of the resounding defeat inflicted on Germany at the end of WWI but also because of the onerous terms of the Treaty of Versailles. It is well known that the terms of the Treaty were extremely harsh, particularly with regard to financial reparations. As a result, the German people soon became imbued with a sense of nostalgia, reminiscing about what the great German Empire used to be. They were pining for a new leader to bring their nation back to its former glory.

They were anxious about what the future held in store for them.

Obviously, these are not exactly the circumstances in which Australia is finding itself today.

Yet, similarly to the uprise of the Nazi movement in 1939, today's emotional distress has created the perfect platform to facilitate the manipulation tactics of the Woke movement.

The movement recruitment tactics are the same as in 1939: the indoctrination of the youth.

The Nazis indoctrinated children into Hitler's Youth movement from the age of ten and put them through a number of programs over a period of eight years, at which time they were

---

[94] Freya Leach, Gen Z's addiction and how to break it; Watercooler newsletter #317, Menzies Research Centre, April 2024.
[95] Jonathan Haidt, The Anxious Generation, Penguin UK, 2024.

then totally conditioned to serve the Fuhrer.

The emphasis was placed on physical fitness and so-called "character". Schools were seen as a waste of time and were required to give up some teaching days so that students could participate in the Hitler Youth movement, also referred to as HJ – Hitler-Jugend.

Hitler created an elite school for Nazi leaders and encouraged young people to attend it. Teachers were burdened with additional extracurricular activities to serve the Third Reich and consequently spent less time in traditional lesson planning and homework marking. Likewise, students had less and less time for school activities. University entrance scores tumbled down.

In the words of the late Professor Daniel Horn,

> *"the false notion that character is superior to intellect, that knowledge and education hardly matter any longer for chaps of irreproachable character... had ruined the receptivity to intellectual values of an entire generation. The shallowness of the HJ's ideology and the manner of its propagation had led students to substitute prejudice and slogans for real "objective education" which they regarded as unnecessary because they felt they already knew all the answers...One instructor, discovering that his students considered Leonardo da Vinci to be an Italian movie star...asked in despair, "How can such people become the intellectual leaders of the new Reich?* [96]

Likewise, nowadays, we are witnessing a significant devaluation of Australia's educational achievements. Our

---

[96] Horn, Daniel. "The Hitler Youth and Educational Decline in the Third Reich." *History of Education Quarterly*, vol. 16, no. 4, 1976, pp. 440-441. *JSTOR*, https://doi.org/10.2307/367724. Accessed 24 Apr. 2024.

teachers are burdened with administrative duties; many change direction or take early retirement, which then creates a shortage of qualified professionals. Some universities lower entry standards to cash in on fees, and curricula are continually restructured to give greater priority to ideology rather than to history.

The Institute of Public Affairs has analysed 3713 teaching subjects in education degrees offered by 37 Australian universities. It has discovered that one third of subjects relate to "woke" theories of identity politics, decolonisation and social justice. Just one in ten relate to teaching children how to read, write and learn mathematics.[97]

Just as the Nazis considered education to be a vehicle for indoctrination, our Australian schools today use all subjects to impart damaging Woke ideology.

In our Australian School Curriculum, ranging from kindergarten to Year 10, indoctrination is rife.

This is facilitated by a number of official cross-curricula priorities that all schools must adhere to, including "Aboriginal and Torres Strait Islander Histories and Culture" at all levels and in all subjects.

For instance, in Year 1, teachers attempt to explain why two plus two equals four through First Nations Australians' dances and in Year 2, the point is hammered home again, using First Nations Australians' stories and dances to understand the balance and connection between addition and subtraction.[98]

Indoctrination is also sustained throughout the high school years: the Institute of Public Affairs recently analysed the reading lists compiled by the Victorian Curriculum and Assessment

---

[97] Bella d'Abrera, Woke unis failing new teachers, The Australian, 22 November 2023.
[98] As reported by Dr Bella D'Abrera, Director of the Institute of Public Affairs in "Dreamtime Maths", The Spectator Australia, 23 March 2024.

Authority and found that most of the 2024 VCE English texts "promote radical identity politics and only six out of thirty-six are from the classic Western canon."[99]

Also, the *Daily Mail* newspaper in the UK reported not long ago that a school made its Australian children write a letter during lesson time, "apologising to the Aboriginal people for the fact that they had **taken** (my emphasis) their land."[100]

Alarmingly, the same "values" the Nazis imparted to the youth of their time are imparted nowadays to our unsuspecting public, but more particularly to our younger generations, for whoever gains the youth owns the future.

For the Nazis, authenticity was primordial. The Nazis had this unfounded belief in an Aryan race, an appellation derived from the Sanskrit term "arya" meaning noble or distinguished. The Nazis thought they were the only true noble race and therefore had a right, even a moral obligation, to purge the world of anything that was not Aryan. Likewise, nowadays, the newly defined oppressed, the black, the transgender, the gay and lesbian and so on are considered to be the true Aryans. They are told that their obligation is to snatch power and supremacy from all Western European culture, especially from white, male and heterosexual oppressors.

As it is the case for the Woke movement, the Nazis also believed in self-care. To survive, you must fight, you must care first of all for the party, for the motherland. The Other does not count, does not deserve care, but rather elimination.

Interestingly, among the key 21st-century virtues, one our children are definitely prone to endorse is "self-care".

---

[99] :Lana Starkey and Morgan Begg, Woke Books on reading list, The Herald Sun, 19th February 2024.
[100] https://www.dailymail.co.uk/news/article-12465619/School-kids-apology-letters-Aboriginal.html (accessed 10/07/2024)

This is particularly so for young girls who are increasingly obsessed by their physical appearance. In the United States, teenagers were spending the equivalent of $324 a year in 2024 on cosmetics, skincare and fragrance, a 23% increase from the previous year, and Australia is not far behind.[101]

Reporter Tansy Hancourt informs us that her 12-year-old daughter has an "elaborate skincare routine" which she undergoes not for the sake of keeping her skin looking young but rather for the sake of the self-care and calming effect and to feel good.[102]

Beauty products have completely invaded social media and this is why they have so much influence among the young. One leading influencer, Sol de Janeiro, is reported to have 1.9 million followers on Instagram and Erika Priscilla is said to have 1.2 million on TikTok.[103]

Are you surprised, dear reader? You should not be: narcissism is a very easy emotion to encourage and reinforce, and what the woke movement conveniently labels self-care is nothing less than a sheer obsession with the self, with the way I look to the world, with my constant concern about the image I project, with my so-called "authenticity".

Besides self-care, the Nazis also used fear to recruit the young: if you are not one of us, you are against us. Likewise, the Woke movement relies on fear to recruit its increasing number of adherents – fear of the future; fear of climate change; fear of being poor; fear of being overlooked by the welfare State and so on.

The Nazis envied the Jews, and this is why they hated them. They envied their economic success, their talent for business and

---

[101] Quoted in the Weekend Australian Magazine, April 13-14 2024, p. 14.
[102] ditto
[103] ditto

their envy grew all the more as their financial situation deteriorated and hyperinflation ravaged Germany. This soon turned into outrage and fuelled resentment and revolt against most of the rest of Europe. Interestingly, as noted earlier on, envy is one of the new 21st-century values, and our youth have become envious of their parent's generation – "Boomer bashing" – envious of their relative economic success and home ownership.

Finally, the Nazis were proud. Proud to be Aryan. Proud to be a true German in the same way as the Woke is proud to be gay, lesbian, black; proud to be anything but white.

Authenticity, self-care/narcissism, envy and pride feature among our 21$^{st}$ century values but they are not new. They were simply "discarded" for a while and now they have resurged; yet our younger generations are historically ignorant and unaware that they are objects of manipulation in the hands of some increasingly ideologically obsessed "elites" whose primary aim is to gain control of their souls, minds and bodies.

## Summary

Compliments of the Woke movement, our children are manipulated to become grenades that, once exploded, become the source of further manipulations, which, in turn, fuel and perpetuate a vicious circle that is hard to break.

Alarmingly, the State manipulates them because the State does not recognise in practice the principle of *locus parentis* which affirms that once parents entrust children to the State for the purpose of a public education, the State should recognise that it is duty bound to abide not by its own values but by the values of those who have chosen their representatives.

Unfortunately, in practice, the State acts as if it owns its youth and inculcates its own dogma. In this way, our children are indoctrinated in a way reminiscent of the tactics of Nazi Germany. Just as the Nazis considered that a good education was first and foremost political in nature, our young generations are currently brainwashed with political messages as early as primary school level.

Indeed, the Australian Curriculum cross priorities focus on the lifestyles of the Aboriginal and Torres Straits Islanders, climate change and the cult of a so-called ethic of "diversity".

As a result, academic scores are tumbling down, just as was the case in Nazis' Germany.

The emotions of pride, fear, and envy featured prominently in the manipulation tactics of the 3rd Reich, and these same emotions are now resurfacing among our youth, albeit in a different context, whilst the perpetrators continue to capitalise on the vulnerability of an anxious generation that is desperately looking for reassurance and new directions.

Even more alarmingly, the search for the authentic that fuelled the Nazis' obsession with preserving their imaginary "pure Aryan race" now drives our young people to embrace a woke philosophy that is bent on achieving purity through the destruction of anything belonging to our past.

# Chapter 9

## Democracy, Sovereignty and the Common Interest

*"We understand hereby that the family, the business, science, art and so forth are all social spheres, which do not owe their existence to the State, but obey a high authority within their own bosom; an authority which rules, by the grace of God, just as the sovereignty of the State does". ~*

Abraham Kuyper.

*"It is a political convention of a democratic society to appeal to the common interest. No political party publicly admits to pressing for legislation to the disadvantage of any recognized social group".*

– John Rawls

The 19th century Dutch Prime Minister Abraham Kuyper, developed the theory known as the "sovereignty of the spheres". Unfortunately, his philosophy has largely been overlooked by 21st-century thinkers on the grounds that Kuyper was a racist and supported the South African apartheid. Although these accusations are justified and proven, nevertheless we should not jettison fully this man's contribution to the important question that continues to vex us today: what limitations should our governments accept vis-à-vis the role they play in our lives?

The question is, indeed, eminently important: our answer to it shall reflect what we understand by democracy.

For Kuyper, the State had a limited sphere of responsibility and was not meant to interfere in all social areas. Unlike our Woke movement that focuses on individual rights for the so-called oppressed, Kuyper focused on the rights of "institutions", such as the trade union movement, the family, the schools, the business sector etc. He saw each of these "institutions" endowed with a particular type of rights or sovereignty that are exclusively theirs and which should not be interfered with by the State authorities; that is to say, the State should not make laws that undermine the relative autonomy granted to these social spheres.

Under the Kuyperian model, the duties of the State are therefore limited and consist of ensuring that each "independent" sphere is not interfering with the autonomy of any of the others, that vulnerable individuals are protected from abuse of power and that citizens make a fair contribution to overall government, for instance, paying their taxes when due and participating actively in the democratic process.

However simplistically foreign this concept of government might sound to our 21st-century ears, some of these key features are not altogether alienated from our Australian federation system with its separate responsibilities allocated to Federal, State and Local branches of government.

Likewise, this system of decentralisation of power is also at the heart of our Western capitalist business model. A Board of Directors may set the direction of the business, but it does not interfere with the day-to-day decision-making, which is entrusted to the executive. Furthermore, the company treasurer does not interfere with the recruitment of staff, and the advertising department does not meddle with recruitment policies; the legal department does not take over the day-to-day decisions of the sales team but provides **support** when required.

Support, here is the key word.

Each sphere is independent and yet, by its own existence, provides support for the proper functioning of the others.

Reverting to our model of society, the educational sphere, therefore, has its own autonomy, but it does function (or should function) by providing support to the family sphere, thus contributing to the preservation of the latter and its autonomy.

The problem with our society nowadays is that its "organisational chart" does not embody a sufficient degree of sophisticated detail to prevent the intrusion of bureaucrats and of our so-called elected representatives into what is really the private sphere, the domain of the family and the individual.

Support is lacking, and intrusion abounds.

How do we then deal with this?

Where do we draw the line? On the one hand, we complain about the intrusion of the State into our private lives but, on the other, we resent the extreme individualism which, for instance, allows genetically born males to participate unfairly in women's sporting events. Do we then need to define sphere sovereignty differently from what Kuyper had in mind? It would seem so, and this should not be altogether surprising since our society has evolved very differently over the last two hundred years.

We are now facing a new existential challenge: the State and the individual are no longer just at odds in the field of economic justice (although this is certainly a factor) but rather in deciding what it means to be human.

In other words, we have regressed; we have lost our way.

Before deciding on the boundaries of the sphere of personal sovereignty, or on the boundaries of the sphere of the family, or on the boundaries of educational authority, or on the limitations of economic justice, we first need to agree on what it means to be human.

If we were to engage in this debate seriously, we would then be leaving the limited scope of this book. Consequently, I do not propose to answer the question of what it means to be human at length.

In any event, others much more qualified than I – such as, for instance, John Lennox and David Gooding[104] – have done so already.

My aim is much more limited and consists simply of stressing that whatever definition we adopt for the word "human", we need to cast it against the background of society at large; in other words, define a human being, not in isolation, but in the context of what being human means in relation to the proper functioning of society in our 21st century.

Currently, the focus is on extreme individualism, and this is leading us into an environment of fragility and isolation, a theme that I have addressed at some length in my former book *Silent, Fragile and Isolated*.

This focus on individualism is not altogether surprising once we realise that our society has been trying for some time now to find meaning to existence through the senses. Reason is no longer a tool to find meaning because Reason leads us to conclude that we cannot ever have all the answers and that, therefore, the ultimate meaning of our existence (in the absence of a belief in the Christian personal God) will always escape us.

Put simply, we foolishly conclude that living through our senses will give us some relief in the face of a world we no longer understand. In fact, more than forty years ago, the American theologian Francis Schaeffer had already reached that same conclusion, but we foolishly ignored it.

---

[104] David Gooding & John Lennox, Being truly human, the limits of our worth, power, freedom and destiny, book 1, the quest for reality and significance, Myrtfield Trust, 2018.

This is what he wrote in 1979:

*"People are hungry for something which will give them hope in life. They are tired of the empty platitudes that politicians and many theologians have made…they are also afraid. Things really do seem hopeless, even on the level of everyday life with its threats of a lower standard of living, of a growing authoritarianism, of famine and ecological disaster, of devastating war. And they are looking for any answer… and so, they believe irrationally… the feeling of experience is enough… it does not matter whether there is any reality to it…people are looking for answers- answers they can experience".[105]*

Is it then little wonder, after all, that an increasing number of people believe there is no such thing as binary gender? Is it really surprising that the reality of Reason (science) no longer applies? Not at all, because what it means to be human is no longer grounded in religious belief or science but only in experience. Experience is the new panacea to the loss of meaning. We do not want to reason, so we experience for the sake of experiencing, and we have no place for people, no place for others; materialistic humanism has led us to become "impersonal".

We cannot continue to live like this.

We need to find a way out.

We need to rediscover if we have, as a nation, a common personal interest.

We need to ask: What does my individual pursuit have in common with the pursuits of society at large?

---

[105] Koop C.E & Schaeffer F.A , Whatever happened to the human race?, Crossway Books, revised edition, 1979.

Expressed another way, what do my thoughts, actions and emotions have in common with those of the rest of society, with what the French pioneer of sociology, Emile Durkheim, called the "social facts"?

If your answer is nothing, then we stay in the impasse. If really, the average Australian has lost any link to the rest of Australian society, then it means there are no longer any "social facts", there are only "individual solitary facts" – in other words, just a mere collection of disassociated individual agents whose goals are foreign to those of our nation as a whole; foreign to the common good.

However, I do not believe we have totally lost our grasp on the common good, on what makes us uniquely Australian, on what binds us rather than on what divides us, but I am concerned that our grasp is no longer strong, in fact, I think it is now so feeble that our fall is imminent.

We are on our way towards the abyss, the Absurd, in other words, towards each of us becoming this Stranger that Albert Camus so brilliantly depicted in his book of the same name.

We are on our way towards it when we allow gender-born males to use gender-born females' toilets or when we allow gender-born males to participate in gender-born female sports. We are on our way towards it when we say: I do what suits me and do not care about the consequences I have on others. We are on our way when our national symbols are attacked, particularly cultural events such as Australia Day. We are on our way towards it when the State refuses to protect the many from the selfish actions perpetrated by the few. We are on our way towards it when power is all we aim for, when destruction becomes the friend and preservation the enemy.

What is left then that binds us together?

What is the common good (singular) and what are our common goods (plural)?

Do we have institutions, facilities that we physically own and that unite us?

These would be our common goods.

Yet, do we also have a morality, a value that we define as good and that binds us together?

That would be our common good, as in good being the opposite of evil.

If you answer "yes" to these questions, then ask yourself two more: what is our common good and how do our common goods work towards achieving it?

Indeed, ask yourself this: what if our common goods, the courts of law, the educational institutions, the parliaments, the police bind us together but against our will and not in the pursuit of the common good?

What happens to us?

Is this not then the end of democracy and the outset of totalitarian rule?

The problem with Australia today is that we place the cart before the horse. We focus on the institutions per se; we think civilisation is achieved once these institutions are in place; we think that our Westminster system of government, with its unique (and yet imperfect) separation of powers, is our guarantee of the preservation of the common good.

A constitutional monarchy might be better than a republic (yes, I know this is an odd remark coming from a French-born male) but it does not protect us if we lose sight of the role of our institutions. If we think our Westminster system of government is enough to preserve our democracy, we are extremely naïve, for this is not so.

Why?

Simply because a constitutional monarchy is only a tool, it is not a solution. The issue is that we no longer know how to use the tool.

We do not know how to use the tool because we are unsure of its purpose. We do not really know what to do with it. We are unsure of what sort of society we want to build.

Yes, I know, this writer and a number of readers are quite sure of what we want to build but the majority of the population does not.

The majority of the Australian population does not bother about a long-term vision for Australia; they do not have the luxury of time to think about it. They are too preoccupied with the cost of living, employment issues, paying off the mortgage and countless other day-to-day challenges. Furthermore, they feel disempowered and unheard. They are the "forgotten ones" who say they no longer bother about these lofty matters because the "elites" do not bother about them.

The fact that we no longer know how to use the common goods available to us for the preservation and growth of our Australian democracy is an important problem we need to resolve.

However, we are also confronted by a second problem: we do not know what the "common good" is anymore because we can no longer agree on what the "common bad" is.

If we could reach a consensus on what our "common bad" is, we could simply say that the "common good" is the antithesis of the "common bad".

Unfortunately, we are so confused, so divided, that we have reached the point where "bad" is now what "good" used to be.

In our endless circular motion to find meaning in our lives, the dot on the clock that indicated "midnight" is now called "midday".

Why are we so confused?

Maybe in part, it is because we are afraid of defining what we really mean by "good"; indeed, this word "good" is a bit of a problem for us because it can soon take a metaphysical sense and in our world, nowadays, metaphysics and religion are thought by many to be the enemy of the good.

Nevertheless, we need to make the effort. Let me ask the question: is there a "common bad"? A common enemy? At first sight, it would seem that there is none.

Yet, interestingly, the word "oppression" keeps popping up.

Admittedly, there is no agreement as to who the victims are. The Woke movement has catalogued a quasi-endless list of identities that it claims to be victims of oppression but, on the other hand, we who are not woke see ourselves as the true victims of a new totalitarianism.

Interestingly, both sides think "oppression" is the common bad.

So, if oppression is the "common bad" (and be it that we differ on the true identity of the victims), can we be at least co-belligerents if we are not to be allies?

If we could at least achieve this much, then there might be a chance to decide where our "common good" lies.

Then, but only then, could we start thinking about how to use our common goods (plural), that is to say, our institutions, to build what we have defined, by consensus, as our common desirable objective, in other words, our common good (singular).

Then and then only can we revisit Kuyper's theory of the spheres and adapt it to our 21st-century Australian society because, at that point, each sphere is not only working to preserve its autonomy but by doing so, it also works for the preservation of the others and therefore the "common good" of our society, taken as a whole.

So, what really is the hurdle? Why is it then so difficult to define the good we would all like to achieve, to own in common?

It is at this point that we discover that unless we understand what it means to be human, we are parked in a dead-end street.

The place of the human in the context of society: I raised the point earlier on but it is so important.

The antonym of oppression is emancipation but emancipation at what price? Does the human come first, or does society come first? This could be a question to raise, but it would be the wrong one. If society comes first, we are going back to utilitarian philosophy with its insistence on the greatest good for the greatest number and history has told us where this leads. On the other hand, if the human comes first and society lasts, then we face the problem that confronts us today: extreme individualism and complete disregard of the Other.

What is the answer then?

It is easier to ask the question than map out the solutions.

Maybe the answer resides in the asking of another question: what sort of society do we want to build? We want democracy but at what price? Do we need to compromise some of it to salvage most of it?

At least we know that democracy cannot be reached or sustained through emotions running supreme. The French Revolution taught us that. In the days of King Louis XVI, the Third Estate – that is, the uneducated masses of the day, the plebeians – had enough of the indulgent excesses of the clergy and the nobility. They were seeking justice, they were seeking recognition, they wanted to be heard, and they could not tolerate being the "forgotten people" anymore.

In itself, there was nothing wrong with this. However, the emotions took over; the negative emotions of anger, hatred, and destruction resulted in anarchy and then oppression, a state of affairs that resulted in the guillotine, a state of affairs that heralded an era known as "The Terror".

Unfortunately, France never recovered from it. It tried hard, tinkering with the experiment of the Empire, going back to the monarchy for a while and then eventually adopting a republican model boasting a slogan of "Liberty, Equality and Fraternity".

However, the jury is now back in, and it would appear that these three words sound somewhat hollow.

France is divided between the extreme left and the extreme right. At the time of writing, no single party has an absolute majority in Parliament and none really wants to compromise.

The class struggle still continues although it has taken a different form, in part due to the arrival of so many immigrants from the former French colonies. A lack of equality also prevails. Yes, it is there "on paper" in the so-called "institutions of the Republic", but too many lack access to the privileges of the few; the "elites" still run supreme.

Most importantly, religion also has lost its place at the table of democracy and the cult of brotherhood (fraternity) has not proven to be a valid substitute.

France is much more secular than Australia. The French boast about the separation of the State and the Church but they took it too far.

Marriages performed by the Church are not recognised by the State and a separate ceremony in front of "Monsieur le Maire" needs to be performed to achieve a recognised union.

There are also very few Christian schools in France, and most of these are Catholic; they represent about 1% of the total of all schools, and these are under contract with the State, which obligates them not to discriminate on the grounds of religion in their student enrolment.[106] [107]

---

106

https://www.google.com/search?q=combien+d%27ecoles+catholiques+sous+contrat+en+fran
ce&rlz=1C1CHZL_enAU763AU763&oq=combien+d%27ecoles+catholiques+sous+contrat+en+fr
ance&gs_lcrp=EgZjaHJvbWUyBggAEEUYOdIBCjI0MTkwajBqMTWoAgCwAgA&sourceid=chrom
e&ie=UTF-8 accessed 20/07/2024

[107] There are about 130 private schools operating without a contract with the Government out of a total of approximately 58000 schools in France. Although they have more freedom to operate than those under contract, they receive no government funding for their payroll

Meanwhile, France is running around in a circle, out of which it does not know how to extricate itself.

Do we really want to reach such a state of affairs? Does Australia want to become another "France"?

Here, I make much of the good of "decentralisation", much about independent spheres retaining their own autonomy and yet, this would not be enough.

France has a form of very decentralised government. A large country by European standards but yet so small in relation to Australia and yet so much decentralisation of power: at the lowest level, the town (la municipalité), then the smaller local area (le département), then the region, then the authorities in Paris.

But does it work?

If you want to create a huge administration, then yes, it does. But if you want to empower *le citoyen,* the individual citizen, results are mixed.

There is a risk of Australia following suit.

Not exactly in the same way but simply with the concept that money and administration are a panacea.

We nearly did it again recently on the occasion of our recent referendum. We nearly built another level of bureaucracy, be it entirely staffed with "first nations people" but bureaucracy all the same. More expenses, more talk fests and still no results.

But what about talking not just among our inner circles but talking face to face, talking to our so-called opponents?

What about stopping being enemies, and if it is too much of a stretch to be allies, at least be co-belligerents in a fight for a better Australia? What about listening? What about showing respect?

As Chris Uhlmann wisely wrote:

> *"we need to articulate a common cause. Here are some*

*thoughts. That all Australians are equal and entitled to equality of opportunity. That we believe in parliamentary democracy and the rule of secular law. That individual rights must be protected by the law and balanced with the common good. That people have the right to practise any form of belief or unbelief as long as they do no harm. And that freedom of speech and a robust media is fundamental to a healthy democracy."*[108]

Yes, I know this sounds simplistic, but we need better answers. Yet it is a beginning, and it is also a good point to begin from.

## Summary

Abraham Kuyper, Dutch Prime Minister and politician, developed a "theory of the spheres", arguing that each class of "institution" in society (for example, the family, business, education sectors etc.) is entitled to a degree of exclusive sphere autonomy and protection from undue interference on the part of the State. For Kuyper, this reduced the role of the State to three principal functions:

a) protecting the intrusion of any institutional sphere into another;

b) protecting and defending vulnerable citizens from any form of abuse of power and,

c) ensuring that citizens fulfil their duty of allegiance to the State, such as paying their taxes and delivering their civic duties.

---

[108] Uhlmann Chris, The War of Ideas, the world changed the moment everyone was able to put the internet in their pocket, The Australian, 60th anniversary collector's edition, July 2024.

Although Kuyper's sphere sovereignty theory never gained much traction in our modern society, some aspects of it are featured in our Australian federation system of governance. It is also illustrated, in part, in the capitalist business model with its delegated model of authority to departments or specialists in such diverse disciplines as, for instance, human relations, legal matters and marketing.

It would be of some benefit to our Australian society if the sovereignty of the spheres model could be adapted to our present situation. This might reduce the present level of excessive intrusion on the part of our governments and bureaucracy into our private spheres, such as the family and education sectors.

Nevertheless, before any of this might proceed, we need to regain some sense of what it means to be human in the overall context of what we mean by society. We need to resolve the tension that currently prevails between the rights of others and the rights of the individual. We must stop thinking that our Westminster system of government (however superior it might be compared to many other forms of polity) is the answer to all our woes. We need to accept, indeed, that our unique Westminster system of government only served us well when we knew it was just a tool and when we knew what the tool was destined to achieve. Unfortunately, we have now forgotten how to use the tool and what we should achieve with it.

We need to discover or rediscover what is our common good or common interest and how to preserve it. If we cannot even unanimously articulate what it is, we are in an impasse or on the edge of an abyss into which we cannot afford to fall.

As a preliminary requirement to any informed debate, we should at least agree that oppression is the "common bad" that both the Woke movement and the rest of our society would like to eradicate. Only once consensus is achieved on this may we then move on towards how we can achieve the "common good" which resides in the simultaneous emancipation of the individual and the preservation of society as a whole.

# Chapter 10

## Democracy and Religion: Allies or Foes?

*"The vanishing point in Western democracies is a loss of faith in its institutions. It is arguable that it starts with the loss of religious faith. But who is the betrayer?"*

(Chris Uhlmann)

*"The Bible is an important part of our culture."*

(Julia Gillard)

Democracy and religion: allies or foes? This is a very topical question, for it seems that, at least in the case of Christianity, the tide might be turning.

Let me explain.

Around twenty years ago, the Western world witnessed the rise of a new movement better known as the New Atheism. The key figures of the New Atheism movement comprised biologist Richard Dawkins, neuroscientist Sam Harris, journalist Christopher Hitchens (now deceased) and philosopher Daniel Dennett (now deceased).

The New Atheists saw all religion as dangerous and primitive. The rise of religious extremism in Islam gave fuel to their arguments, and the events of 9/11 galvanised them.

They explained the universe as all humanists do, that is, in terms of humanistic materialism. The spiritual nature does not exist – only matter exists. We are all spiritless molecules.

However, their influence is waning. The rise of the Woke movement has split the left-of-centre intellectual world. Much of the demise of the New Atheism seems to spring from Richard Dawkins' persistent invitations to insult and ridicule Christian believers.

His aggressive manner has resulted in him being accused of misogyny, sexism and male privilege.

In the words of leading Christian public intellectual, Justin Brierley:

> *"the fallout from the controversies that have circled Dawkins and other leading atheists has revealed the deep rifts at the core of atheist communities".*[109]

As a result, the Bible is under scrutiny again: we are now witnessing the rise of a new type of agnostics who might not classify themselves as believers but are attracted by the values of the New Testament Bible. Leading public intellectuals such as Jordan Peterson, Douglas Murray and Jonathan Haidt are at the forefront of the rise of a sort of "Christian atheism".

Consequently, it would be very culturally relevant and timely to ask whether Christianity is the friend or foe of democracy.

In fact, it is quite opportune now to ask if religion (not just Christianity) is generally the friend or foe of democracy.

However, allow me to backtrack for a few moments.

My personal motivation in writing this book has been my passion for freedom of speech, religious expression and democracy.

Freedom of speech is one of the marks of a civilised, mature people and democracy cannot exist without at least some degree of freedom of speech and religious expression.

---

[109] Brierley J, The surprising rebirth of belief in God, Tyndale, 2023

At its very core, democracy is the power of the people: from the Greek "demos", "the people" and "kratia", "power or rule": "démokratia". Admittingly, the rule of the people is not necessarily a good rule, and a plethora of historical events proves it; nevertheless, there are more chances of better outcomes when power is shared by the many rather than when jealously guarded by the few.

I believe that men and women of faith play an important role in the development and preservation of democracy.

I share the opinions of the Jordan Petersons of this world, and I am convinced that it is wrong to believe that religion is always the enemy of democracy.

Michelle Bachelet, a former United Nations High Commissioner for Human Rights, agreed with me when she wrote:

> *"Human rights and faith can be mutually supportive. Indeed, many people of faith have worked at the heart of the human rights movement, precisely because of their deep attachment to respect for human dignity, human equality, and justice".*

> *"I am convinced that faith-based actors can promote trust and respect between communities. And I am committed to assisting governments, religious authorities and civil society actors to work jointly to uphold human dignity and equality for all".*[110]

The real challenge, however, is not simply to accept that religion and democracy can have some sort of peaceful co-existence but that religion can provide added value to the state

---

[110] https://www.ohchr.org/EN/Issues/FreedomReligion/Pages/FaithForRights.aspx (accessed 15.6.2024)

of our democracy in Australia and, therefore, become an ally to democracy.

Admittedly, in a democratic society, not all opinions are valid, not all viewpoints are wise, and not all declarations are helpful; indeed, many are quite wrong, many quite foolish, and quite a few are very ineffective. Likewise, not all religious practices are wise, helpful and constructive. Some might even be abusive.

Yet, this is not the point.

The point is that in a democracy, and precisely because not all viewpoints are true, religion should have a seat at the discussion table.

Many will disagree. I am under no illusion. In spite of the renewed interest shown in the Christian bible by the new "cultural Christians" many will say that the Christian Church has lost its right to come to the discussion table because of the abuse it has perpetrated in the past, and some of it even in the very recent past.

Yet, this is wrong. Democracy is not the union of the custodians of truth. Rather, it is the process from which we hope truth shall emerge. As C.S Lewis wrote: "The reason for democracy is that mankind is so fallen that no one can be trusted with unchecked power over his fellows".[111]

Since religion claims to have much to contribute about truth, it follows that religion should have a seat at the table of democracy so that we, together, the people, may discern and agree on what is true, noble and effective to run our society harmoniously.

However, when I mention religion, I mean religion with a capital R – in other words, not just that set of beliefs restricted to a particular faith but rather, religion in the broader sense of

---

[111] C.S Lewis. "Equality" in "Present Concerns" quoted in Christopher Watkin (2022), p.119

the term to include most forms of religious belief.

I say "most" because, under some religious systems, democracy is considered to be the archenemy of society. These religions are simply theocratic and are clearly opposed to democracy.

Given that qualification, I believe it is counterproductive to exclude any particular faith from the table of democratic discourse simply because it is considered not to be worthy of it.

Deciding that the broader Christian church is no longer "good enough" to be accepted because of its long record of abusive behaviour is wrong because it denies the essence of democracy: freedom of speech and freedom of belief. Furthermore, and ironically, it, in fact, opens the door to the very thing foes of religion oppose: a new type of theocracy.

Indeed, if Religion is altogether barred from access to the table of democratic discourse, we have maybe, unwittingly, replaced our belief in a Divine Being, an immemorial, quasi-universal belief in a non-human God, with one in a new God of blood and flesh, carved in our own image: the foundation of a new form of theocracy.

Tragically, this would mean that we have then pushed our humanistic religion so far that all beliefs would need to conform to the new edicts of the great priests of the new Human God. Traditional faiths and religious creeds would be barred from their forms of "living faith" applications in day-to-day situations.

Our entire way of life would then bow to this religion, and the State would be in a position where it could treat any so-called breaches of this new man-made faith with the full force of the law.

I say "could" but, in some ways, I might stand corrected and accept that I should say "can" because, to a significant extent, this is already happening: the great priests of this new Human God are none other than our ruling "elites".

They reject the right that persons of faith have with regard to the type of education they want to impart to their children, they reject the right persons of faith have in the selection of staff in religious schools, they reject the right persons of faith have to oppose abortion and euthanasia; as a matter of fact, they reject anything that does not fall within the narrow confines of their totalitarian ideology; even at times, the very right to pray, the right of reply, the right to speak.

My concern, indeed, is that we have now reached the stage where the fear or contempt of religious practices and belief has had the perverse effect of heralding a new type of manmade religion: humanism.

The very foundations of our Australian political system are threatened by the rise of woke humanism.

Our system of government is based on the British Westminster parliamentary system. It offers a great advantage: it is anchored in Christian religious belief.

We were recently reminded of this at the coronation of Charles III. Unfortunately, we are now gradually opting for a constitutional monarchy without a place for God.

Eventually, this will lead us to adopt a republican model, an Australian form of Liberty, Equality and Fraternity and French contemporary history is showing us where this leads.

The Christian church is part of the institutions on which Australia was founded, and the crisis we experience today is the result of a loss of faith in our institutions and, therefore, a loss of faith in the added value the Christian church can offer to society.

How should we then deal with this?

Let us start by looking at what divides us nowadays, namely wokeism.

Let us examine what it is tied to, and we shall find that on the one hand, wokeism is bound up with collectivism, from the union catch-cry of "the workers will never be divided" to the insistence that all gay/black/young/conservative/atheist or any other prescribed identity grouping all think the same and want the same.

Yet, on the other hand. the woke movement is also firmly anchored in the pursuit of individualism. It wants to preserve individual liberties for its adherents at the expense of the rest of society.

It is a futile pursuit. It is anti-democratic.

The woke movement cries out that Christianity is the enemy of democracy whilst, in fact, it is the reverse: Christianity is not inimical to democracy but the woke movement is.

Christianity and many other religions are anchored in community – wokeism is not.

After all, it was the early Christian missionaries who built many of our hospitals and schools in this country and it is also thanks to countless number of Christian charities that we still have the not-for-profit sector encompassing aged care facilities, private schools and street aid organisations.

The common factor for all of these charities and missions is, indeed, care for the community but let us remember that what preserves any community is the presence of democracy.

Without democracy, a community can no longer function because, without democracy, the decisions that are made are no longer made in common with the many but rather imposed by the few.

The woke movement sees the Christian religion as the enemy of individualism but the beauty of Christianity is that it can blend both individualism and community into one.

Indeed, it is because the Christian faith is so much anchored into community that it can elevate the status of the individual. Far from being suppressed by the rule of the Christian community, the individual is upheld, elevated and honoured in traditional Christian practice.

Modern Christianity is no theocracy. The theocratic model presented in the Old Testament was only relevant to that period of history which preceded the death and resurrection of Jesus Christ. The legalism of the Old Testament and its associated type of punishments (stoning, etc.), its misunderstood application on the part of the so-called Old Testament, "experts in the law" of those times have now given way to a new understanding of the place of humanity in the world and our relationship to God.

Under a *Christian* model of government, the individual is not repressed but rather uplifted because, at its core, Christian theology holds that humans are made in God's image.

Hence, Christianity harbours a form of individualism, but it is kept in its proper place, so to speak. It is not a free-for-all selfish type of individualism where one might decide anything he or she wants, irrespective of the consequences on the rest of society. It is individualism that respects the Other, individualism that respects democracy.

It is individualism that adds value, not subtract or deny or impair. It is liberating, emancipating and caring.

There is, however, another major obstacle to Christianity playing its part in building up a democratic Australia. This obstacle is "within" the Christian community. It is nothing else than many of the churches themselves.

At times, the Christian churches are their worst enemy because they refuse to come to the discussion table of democracy. They are scared of involvement in politics. They come up with the usual feeble excuse that politics divide and that politics are stained, impure and have a corrupting influence.

There is also, among some of the clergy, the belief that the role of the Church, an institution, is to preach, whilst that of the churchgoers is to put the preaching into action. Although there is some merit in this position, the practical outcome of it is that some churches do not even preach any form of political involvement, even on those themes where the Bible is transparently clear, such as, for instance, the issue of abortion. So, when a hospital run by Catholic nuns, opposed to abortion, was forcibly taken over by the Australian Capital Territory, some Christian churches refused to resort to any form of official communication which might have encouraged their parishioners to reflect on the matter and resort to peaceful political protest.

This is a significant issue because reality dictates that we very much need to enlist the faithful involvement of **all** democratically oriented Australians at the grassroots level. To protect freedom of religion, to protect its very existence as a visible, high-profile institution, the Christian church should encourage all of its members to fight for their beliefs.

The problem is that not only a great many of the *forgotten people* are disenchanted about politics and therefore disengaged, but also a great many of our churchgoers avoid political involvement altogether. Sadly, the few who do not are barred from publicly declaring their stance by a clergy overwhelmingly concerned with the potential threat of dividing their flock.

Some denominations even go as far as refuting that they are "churches". The Church of England, for instance, is considering renaming itself by dropping the epithet of "church" and replacing it with 'community". With such fear of being pigeonholed under the appellation of "church", with such misplaced shame in what the Christian church has brought to the world, how should then Christians participate in the political process? What should they do to preserve democracy, to protect their right to speak, their right to object, their right to participate?

The answer is obvious: simple individual involvement, starting with voting for people who represent the values of the voters, rather than for parties; in other words, voting for those who will have the courage to stand up and to hold the so-called "elites" to account.

This is the first step. It is foundational. Vote for the person, not the party.

Secondly, there is a need to speak out between elections, the need, for instance, to join a lobby group that will represent the values persons of faith want to uphold, the need to attend conferences, rallies – in other words, the need to stay informed. Finally, there is a need to contact your local Member of Parliament to express your view, even if it is only through a petition.

There is, therefore, a role for people of faith, particularly Christians, to play a part in the defence of democracy in Australia, a role that the institutional Christian church should encourage without being particularly party-based.

But there is also more. Christians need to avoid approaching the culture of the day with black-and-white lenses. Or, in the words of University of Cambridge Christopher Watkin:

> *"if Christians approach our culture with the aim of denouncing or humiliating it, they are unlikely to make any impact, will almost never bring healing, and are more at risk of not recognising where their own thoughts and instincts are more cultural than biblical. Similarly, if they approach our culture only with the goal of affirming or even praising it, they are signing up for biblical unfaithfulness and cultural irrelevance".*[112]

Expressed another way, religion (and in this particular instance, I mean Christianity) should be asking questions of the

---

[112] Christopher Watkin, Biblical Critical Theory, Zondervan Academic, 2022, p.27.

current culture in a way that leads our contemporaries to reflect.

Interestingly, the woke movement is brandishing values that are, at their core, essentially Christian (for instance, justice, love and compassion), but it redefines them and reclothes them into a strange apparel that completely changes what they are meant to be.

Let us then underline these values and show that the way Christians understand them is, in fact, the key to fulfilling the quest of the woke movement: justice for the oppressed.

We need to deconstruct the woke mentality.

We also need to appreciate that the cultural conflict we are immersed in is not simply "conservative" versus so-called "progressive". It is a clash of culture of cosmic proportions. It is more than woke against non-woke. It is a war against the West conducted by a number of parties who would never dream of being allies but just find themselves sharing a co-belligerent status against Western civilisation.

I mean, the gay, the transgender and all those who find their niche somewhere in the collective of the LGBTQA+ brand could never be the proper allies of the Hezbollah and Hamas militants who oppose any form of cultural and religious diversity.

Yet, both are enemies of Israel, and they are not interested in the land as such but rather in the destruction of the Jewish people for the same reasons they wish to destroy Christianity and all this religion stands for.

Dear reader, be under no illusion: the leaders of Hezbollah and Hamas, and Iran are not just fighting for the destruction of Israel: they are fighting against the entire value system of the Western world.

In this sense, what is happening in Australia is simply a microcosm of the conflict raging between Eastern and Western cultures. In this sense, it is already a world war.

So, what should we do?

If general objections to Christian beliefs are grounded in a culture opposing the Eastern and Western cultures, we need to identify them. These defeater beliefs vary over time and vary between cultures.

In some Muslim countries, belief in Christianity is defeated by considering that "turning the other cheek" or "giving one's tunic as well" are weak. These are Christian edicts that have no place in cultures that see war as a means to religious conquest.

Conversely, in the West, the present "garden variety" of defeater beliefs largely promotes the view that the Christian faith restricts freedom of action and freedom of speech. Christianity is a straitjacket! How ironical! The very thing Christianity opposes is that which it is accused of.

How do we deal with this? The late Timothy Keller argued that we do not necessarily need to "answer" these beliefs to the fullest extent but at least deconstruct them to show that the Christian message is a viable alternative.

> *"Our purpose with these defeaters or doubts is…to show that they are not as solid or as natural as they first appear…it is important to show that all doubts and objections to Christianity are really alternate beliefs and faith-acts about the world…and when you see your doubts and beliefs and require the same amount of evidence for them that you are asking of Christian beliefs, then it becomes evident many of them are very weak, and largely adopted because of culture pressure".[113]*

---

[113] Keller Tim, Deconstructing Defeater Beliefs, Leading the Secular to Christ https://www.goodsoil.com/docs/DeconstructingDefeaterBeliefs.pdf (accessed 13/09/2024)

The challenge is, therefore, threefold: firstly, engage into the culture in a way that shows sympathy for those who labour under a burden of fear, isolation, injustice and prejudice; secondly break the indifference, fear and discouragement in some sections of the Christian church, and thirdly, engage into a dialogue that replaces the tyranny of the woke emotions with the truth, goodness and beauty of the Gospel.

The woke movement is fully committed to a never-ending celebration of its own values: its Pride Days, its Purple Days, its NADOC Days and so on.

So, what about Christianity? If celebration is cultural, why not celebrate what Christianity can offer? If emotions are part of the Australian contemporary cultural make-up, why not use them? The title of this book is "Emotional manipulation: an assault on our democracy", but this does not mean all emotions are bad.

Christopher Watkin, again:

> *"A Christian engagement with truth, goodness, or beauty that does not end in praise is missing something, like visiting the Venice opera and spending the entire performance studying the program".114*

Let me clarify. When I say "praise", I do not think of the celebratory worship style of many of our Christian churches, the singing, the Halleluiahs, the raising of hands. There is some place for this, but if we are speaking of addressing the culture of the day, what we do behind the closed doors of our sanctuaries is not going to make any difference. Therefore, when I am talking about praise, I am talking about a public lifestyle, a way of engaging in everyday life that shows that Christianity has the answers to the objections raised by the woke movement.

Our culture wants to restrict Christianity to worship practices

---

114 Christopher Watkin, Biblical Critical Theory, p.602.

behind closed doors, yet Christianity is all about changing lives; it is a praising lifestyle because it majors on the positives. The culture of our day, in particular that of the woke movement, focuses on the negatives. It speaks about oppression, injustice, invasion, and discrimination, and really, it has little to rejoice about. Christianity, on the other hand, speaks about liberation, sanctification, acceptance, forgiveness, joy and peace. This is why it should have an important seat at the table of democracy. Without it, the emotions of the culture of the day are simply tools in the hands of the manipulating elites.

## Summary

An opportunity now exists for people of faith, and more particularly Christians, to be heard. The demise of the New Atheism movement and the resulting splintering of the humanist Left has created an opportunity for a number of well-articulated public intellectuals to examine the values of the Bible and the relevance of their application to the defence of our democracy.

It is important, however, that this renewed interest in matters spiritual starts by recognising that most people of faith do not aspire to a return to theocracy, which, by definition, is the foe of democracy.

With the exception of some specific faiths, religious believers aspire to uphold freedom, equality and respect for all. They, therefore, believe in the tenets of democracy.

The argument that the Christian church has lost its right to come to the "table" of discussion of democracy is spurious. It also contradicts the woke alleged commitment to inclusion.

In any society, any party that supports the concept of democracy should be entitled to participate in the political process by defending freedom of expression, decision-making, and religious belief.

It follows, therefore, that any faith group that does not aspire to the maintenance or return of a theocratic state should be welcome to the discussion table.

The sad reality that a significant portion of the Christian church has been tainted by the horror of abuse should not be a bar to participation in the democratic process. Democracy is not the union of blameless truth custodians but simply the process by which the best decisions can be made for the benefit of all Australians, not just for favoured groups.

An engagement in politics on the part of the Christian church, if properly construed, has nothing to do with a return to theocracy.

However, for the church to be an ally to democracy, it requires people of faith to accept that if politics are "darkness", the Church has all the more reason to be involved, to be an agent of "light". For the average Australian church goer, it would mean becoming engaged personally in the political process with a view of making a difference and regaining the ground presently lost to the Woke movement.

It would mean addressing the culture of the day in a way that avoids throwing the baby out with the bathwater; at the same time, it would mean that the Church is courageous and does not seek popularity by redefining itself in such a way as to lose its true authenticity.

It would mean publicly focusing on the true emotions that inspire genuine praise, those that arise from beauty and truth.

It would mean majoring in the Christian understanding of liberation, sanctification, acceptance, forgiveness, joy and peace.

Or, in the words of leading Australian theologian Mark Durie [115]:

---

[115] Mark Durie, Right, Left and the Politics of Time: A Christian response (Markdurie.com) accessed 26/10/2024

*"The enduring challenge for politically aware, engaged Christians is to find new and fresh ways to speak the truth into the world... We must resist the temptation to hitch our theologies to the spirit of the age or to either side of politics. We must not replace faith in a God who saves human beings from sin... with either a naïve belief in progress or a dependence upon deeply flawed social and cultural traditions of the past. We must allow our political vision to be constantly tested, reformed and renewed by the values of the gospel of Jesus Christ".*

This is, indeed, the message that the Christian church, as an institution, needs to promote.

# Conclusion

## Whither goes thou?

*Love the god of wokeness with all your heart soul and mind and shame the white as much as you love yourself. The whole demise of the Western world hangs on these two commandments.*

This book raises more questions than it provides answers.

The reason for this has partly been deliberate on my part: the average Australian needs to "press Pause" and take some time to reflect and start asking the questions that matter; pondering on how, at our individual level, in our given set of circumstances, with our given set of gifts and talents, we can participate in finding the answer to the great challenge of our time: *how can we nurture, protect and enhance the state of our democracy in this great land of ours?*

How can we make sure that we are no longer children, tossed to and fro by every wind of doctrine, by human cunning, by craftiness in deceitful schemes?

We cannot afford to be a mere pendulum responding to emotional pressures that swing us either to the left or right of the political divide.

We need to find stable ground and to do so, seriously ask the fundamental question of how then we shall live.

Of course, this question was asked by other much more learned persons in the past.

Nevertheless, we can and should ask the same questions but seek, more than ever, an answer we can all adopt, that is to say, not just for people of faith but for all Australians, irrespective of birth, privilege, skin colour or education.

We need to come up with an answer that speaks to our current culture, not to the cultures of the past, not to those of our parents or grandparents, but to our contemporary culture. Our answer may, therefore, be different from what was given in the past because circumstances have changed, but the truth of our reply should not change; the way we communicate it might only be different. Above all, our answer needs to unite, to rally towards the common good. Currently, the answers given simply foster division and resentment because they do not seek out the truth.

The quest for this eluding answer should start with the recognition that our better judgment is currently clouded by emotions that lead us astray. We need to extricate ourselves from this dominion of the "feelings" and regain the intellectual composure that we have lost.

The present culture war against the West is not unlike that of school bullies. Where does the hatred of a bully come from? Usually not from anything the target victim says or does but purely from the pleasure of inflicting harm. One thing bullies do and do well: they choose their victims carefully. They make sure they are not strong boys or girls who have the confidence to stand up to them. This is also, unfortunately, what is happening to our Western culture. We have become so weak and so hesitant, so unsure of ourselves that we are now presenting ourselves as prime targets to all those who are jealous of what we have accomplished to date, all those who hate law and order, reward for hard work, and the Judeo-Christan values on which our society stands.

Our opponents know that this bullying cannot succeed by relying on reason and on an accurate rendering of our historical past: the classroom bully often picks on bright kids and proceeds to destroy them through emotional harassment, not through an intellectual debate that he cannot possibly win.

This is what is happening to the West; our opponents know that they cannot win the war through reasonable argument, through a meeting of the minds, so they focus on emotional warfare, creating false guilt, false shame and false love.

The whole world is now immersed in ideology. Whether it is the communism of China and North Korea, the territorial imperialism of Russia or the woke culture of the West, emotions drive the philosophies of the nations of the world.

We need to resist this war of emotions. We need to learn to discern, not just with our hearts, but with our minds and souls too. We need to revisit the dangers present in that intensification of emotions people experience during collective rituals and mass protests. The French sociologist Emile Durkheim wrote about this last century under the label of "collective effervescence," and maybe he was already sounding a warning to us at the time, which we conveniently ignored.

We need to relearn the basics of love and respect.

Most importantly, we need to start discovering what it really means to be human, for without that basic knowledge, how may we ever aspire to define the true power of the people, democracy?

Is the average Australian even aware of being constantly manipulated by both the political parties and the "elites" of our land? Are we aware that we are gradually giving in to a new mindset that challenges all we have cherished in the past? Are we aware that the Woke movement is not the answer to freedom but the beginning of a new slavery?

We could say that many of us have given up on fighting for democracy. We have become disengaged, and the Christian church, once a bastion of our culture, is also now disengaged.

This cannot be. We need a new brand of leaders, teachers, judges, legislators, and law enforcers.

As a nation, we need to re-examine what it means to be "virtuous".

As I am putting the final touches to this manuscript, the conflict between Israel and Hamas has amplified: Iran is now at war with Israel, and the world, including Australia, seems quite happy to abandon the Jewish people. Universities tolerate, if not facilitate, a degree of anti-Semitism not previously displayed in this country, and, even worse, the government, the police and the army appear to support it.

I cannot fathom what the motivation is for such a display of hatred except that many, and not just our youth, are manipulated to an extent unknow to date in Australia.

Hence, we jump in before we think. We have become both manipulators and manipulated.

Even some of our institutions, which, at face value, appear to be bastions of truth, organisations professing a mission anchored in the dignity of the individual, now seem to uphold double standards. Take, for instance, the example of the Australian Catholic University (ACU).

A cursory glance at its website informs us that the ACU stands for the dignity of the individual.

> *"At ACU, our mission is our difference. Through the lens of the Catholic intellectual tradition, acting in Truth and Love, we are committed to* **human dignity***, the pursuit of knowledge and the* **common good***".* (bold lettering is my emphasis).

Yet, when Joe de Bruyn, a well-known Catholic and Australian union leader, was awarded an honorary PhD by ACU, most of the faculty and the students walked out upon hearing his views condemning abortion and upholding the value of human life.[116]

Why is all this happening?

May I say that part of the answer is probably because we have redesigned education to be either the acquisition of specific skills for a trade (in other words, training) or the acquisition of a philosophy that pushes the woke agenda from primary school to university and beyond.

Yet, this is not what education is meant to achieve. The Latin etymology for the word "education" means to bring up or bring forth. Education is neither training nor indoctrination. Teaching has a much nobler purpose and that is to make us discover what virtuous living is all about.

Bring forth virtuous living!

We need to teach "thinking" that promotes virtuous living!

Thinking should be a school subject!

In my high school days, we were taught the art of writing a dissertation, or essay writing if you prefer. We were given a quote and a sentence from a well-known author, and we were asked to write a one- or two-thousand-word essay on it. For instance, Edmond Haraucourt's *"to leave is to die a little"* or René Descartes' *"I think therefore I am"*. Alternatively, we were given a topic, such as the dignity of man in the midst of the machine world or the value of education.

The purpose was to make us think and think deeply. We were fourteen, fifteen and sixteen years old. We were at the age where we were no longer children and not yet adults – the age where

---

[116] As reported in the Weekend Australian, 26-27 October 2023 under the title "Axis of ill will be emboldened by the West's weakness"

thinking becomes primordial – the age where emotions cannot be let loose without restraint.

Why do we not teach this in Australia?

Why is school education all about indoctrination rather than free thinking?

Why do we no longer value the thoughts and wisdom of those who preceded us?

Why is it that the pursuit of all knowledge has now given way to feeling a particular way?

It is not even sufficient for our universities to pepper all their courses with reference to the new woke dictum: they go further and provide diplomas and degrees in diversity and the like. The University of Melbourne, for instance, has an Associate Dean Diversity and Inclusion and an Associate Dean Indigenous as well as a "People of Colour" department. Furthermore, the University does not appear to encourage hard work and success: its Australian Centre does not relate stories of Australian migrants' success and assimilation on the grounds that this would detract from the emphasis it places on the struggling and persecuted migrant minorities!

We need to put an end to this nonsense.

We need to dismantle the ten new Woke "virtues" of our 21st century and denounce them for their inconsistency and for the oppressive values they harbour. For indeed, how do you justify, on the one hand, talking about dying with dignity and choosing one's "exit" time but on the other hand, placing babies born alive after failed abortions into witches' hats, unattended, abandoned to die, struggling on their own, sometimes up to five hours without medical care?[117]

---

[117]At the time of writing, the only Australian states that provide legislative protection for baby survivors of abortion are New South Wales and South Australia. A motion introduced in 2024 into the Senate by United Australia

The woke movement wants autonomy, that is, the capacity to regulate itself independently, without constraint, in a search for the ever-elusive authentic self.

For the woke, autonomy means dignity.

How foolish! There is no dignity where there is conflict and destruction.

Do they not understand that a total focus on autonomy calls for the continuation of the very conflict the movement sets out to denounce?

Autonomy, as understood by the woke movement, brings the absence of peace, of *shalom*, so it is, in fact, far from being virtuous.

Or as Christopher Watkin so eloquently puts it:

> "*autonomy is inherently conflictual…if no necessary authority greater than me or outside me can challenge my own lawmaking, and if no such authority resides outside you either, then fundamental differences between us cannot be settled in a nonpartisan and irenic way. The only way to resolve conflict is on the basis of power, either naked power (we fight each other, and one of us becomes the slave to the other's master) or sublimated power…we both choose to submit to a common rule backed by brute force*".[118]

The challenge for Australia is therefore not just sociological, nor merely political: it is really existential for we have moved even beyond the stage of democratic backsliding: we have reached the stage of quasi permanent division and conflict.

---

senator, Ralph Babet, seeking to protect survivors of abortion through the use of the external affairs power was lost after all votes were counted.
[118] Watkin (2022), p.146

As Ronald Reagan once said:

> *"Freedom is never more than one generation away from extinction. We didn't pass it to our children in the bloodstream. It must be fought for, protected and handed on for them to do the same, or one day we will spend our sunset years telling our children and our children's children what it was once like in the United States where men were free".*

The same warning applies to us here in Australia

# Bibliography

Acemoglu D & Robinson J.A: The Rise and Decline of General Laws of Capitalism, Journal of Economic Perspective, Vol. 29, No 1- Winter 2015, p 3-28.

Arendt H: Truth & Politics, the New Yorker, Feb. 25 1967.

Babones S: The New Authoritarianism, Polity Press 2018.

Baucham V.T. Jnr: Fault Lines, Salem Books 2021/

Benkler Y et al: Network Propaganda, Manipulation, Disinformation and Radicalization in American Politics, Oxford University Press, 2018.

Berry J & Sobieraj S: The Outrage industry, Political Opinion, Media and the New Incivility, Oxford University Press, 2013.

Bondar G: Silencing of the Lambs, Connor Court 2022.

Borgos A et al: Psychology and politics; Intersection of Science and Ideology in the History of Psy-Sciences; Central European University Press 2019.

Bradshaw S & Howard P.N: Challenging Truth and Trust: a Global Inventory of Organised Social Media Manipulation, University of Oxford, 2018.

Brierley J: The Surprising Rebirth of Belief in God, Tyndale, 2023.

Bruckner P: The Tyranny of Guilt, Princeton University Press, English translation 2010.

Campbell & Manning: The Rise of Victimhood Culture, Palgrave McMillan, 2018.

Case A & Deaton A: Deaths of Despair and the Future of Capitalism, Princeton University Press, 2021.

Castell M: Networks of Outrage and Hope; Social Movements in the Internet age; edition 2, John Wiley@ Sons 2015.

Chavura C et al: Reason, Religion and the Australian Polity, A Secular State? Routledge 2019.

Crouch C: Post Democracy After the Crisis, Polity Press, 2020.

Evans & Stone A: Open Minds, Australian Freedom and Freedom of Speech in Australia, La Trobe University Press, 2021.

Flint D & Martinkovits J: Give us back our country; Connor Court, 2013.

Fontana Stefani: Permeating the Human Psyche: the role of emotions in nazi propaganda; School of Humanities & Communicating Arts, Western Sydney University 2021.

Fredheim Rolf et al: Social Media Manipulations 2022-2023; assessing the ability of social media companies to combat platform manipulation; NATO Strategic Communications Centre for Excellence, 2023.

Furedi F: How Fear Works, Culture of Fear in the 21st Century, Bloomsbury, 2018.

Furedi F: 100 Years of Identity Crisis, Culture War over Socialisation, De Gruyter 2021.

Furedi F: Where have all the intellectuals gone (2nd ed.) Bloomsbury 2004.

Ghia N: The End of Postnational Illusion; Journal of Democracy, Vol. 28, no 2, April 2017.

Giusti S & Piras E: Democracy and Fake News: information manipulation and post truth politics, Routledge 2020.

Goldsworthy J: Losing Faith in Democracy, Quadrant, 2015

Golles D: The Man Who Broke Capitalism; Simon & Schuster, 2022.

Gooding D & Lennox J: Being Truly Human, Myrtlefield Trust, 2018

Goodwin M: Values, Voice & Virtue: the new British politics, Random House, 2023.

Grube D.C: Megaphone Bureaucracy: speaking truth to power in the age of the new normal, Princeton University Press 2019.

Gruning D.J: Schubert T.W: Emotional Campaigning in Politics, Heidelberg University, Heidelberg, Germany, 2022.

Guilluy C: Twilight of the Elites: prosperity, the periphery and the future of France, (English translation), Yale University Press, 2019.

Habermas J: The Postnational Constellation; Political Essays, John Wiley & Sons, 2018.

Haidt J: The Righteous Mind, Penguin UK, 2012.

Haidt J: The Anxious Generation, Randow House, 2024.

Hanson V.D: The Dying Citizen: how progressive "elites", tribalism and globalization are destroying the idea of America; Hachette UK, 2021.

Harari Y.N: Homo Deus, a Brief History of Tomorrow, Random House, 2016.

Healy Andrew J et al: Personal emotions & political decision making; implications for voter competence; Research Paper Series, Research Paper 2034, Stanford Graduate School of Business July 2009.

Heller H: The Birth of Capitalism, a 21st century perspective, Pluto Press, Jstor, downloaded from 60.242.206.155, 29.06.2023.

Hellwig M: Capitalism: what has gone wrong? Oxford Review of Economic Policy, Vol. 37, No 4, p. 664-667, 2021.

Hendershott A: The Politics of Envy, Sophia Institute Press 2020.

Hickman C et al: Young People's Voices on Climate Anxiety, The Lancet Planetary Health, Issue 12, 863-877, Dec. 2021.

Jacobs A: How to think, A Guide for the Perplexed, Profile Books, 2018.

Jaquenod P: Silent Fragile and Isolated, Linellen Press, 2022

Johns G: The Burden of Culture, Quadrant Books 2023.

Joustra J & Joustra R et al: Calvinism for a Secular Age, Intervarsity Press, 2022.

Katz J & Mays K: Journalism and Truth in an Age of Social Media, Oxford University Press, 2019.

Keller T: Making Sense of God, Hodder & Stoughton, 2016.

Klimo v, Arpad: Nazi Discourses on « Rausch » Before & After 1945, Codes & Emotions, UCLA Working Papers, University of California, 20/12/2004.

Koop C.E & Schaeffer F.A: Whatever happened to the human race? Crossway, rev. edition, 1979 and 1983.

Kramer G: The Apathetic Country; why ignorant voters dominate Australian politics; Austin Macauley, 2023.

Kurke A et al: The Human Right to Democratic Control of Artificial Intelligence, Report to Australian Human Rights Commission, April 2020.

Lennox J.C: 2084: Artificial intelligence & the future of humanity, Zondervan 2020.

Lind M: The New Class War, Atlantic Books, 2020.

Lukianoff G & Haidt J: The Coddling of the American Mind, Penguin Books, 2018.

Marcellino W et al: Generative AI & the coming era of social manipulation 3.0; Rand Corporation, 2023.

Marcus G.E: Emotions in Politics, Annu. Rev. Politi Sci. 2003.3: 221-50.

Miranda J.M & Aldea A: Emotions in Human & Artificial Intelligence, Computers in Human Behaviour 321-341, 2005.

McStay A & Rosner G: Emotional Artificial Intelligence in children's toys and devices; Ethics, Governance and Practical Remedies, Big Data & Society, Sage Publications January-June 1-16, 2021.

Modood T: Multiculturalism, Polity Press, 2013 (2nd ed).

Moran A: Globalisation, Postnationalism and Australia, Journal of Sociology 2021, Vol.57(1) 128-145, Sage Publications.

Moskovsky C: "It keeps pointing left", IPA Review, Volume 75/2, p.52-54. Institute of Public Affairs Ltd, Melbourne.

Moens, G.A: Culture of Conformity Makes it Difficult to Defeat the Voice, Spectator Australia, 9 October 2023.

Murray D: The War on the West, Harper Collins, 2022.

Noggle R: Manipulation in Politics in Oxford Research Encyclopedia of Politics, Oxford University Press, Sept 29, 2021.

Orwell G: Politics and the English Language, Penguin UK, 2013.

Peterson J.G: Beyond Order, 12 More Rules for Life, Penguin Books, 2021.

Piper J: Bloodlines, Race, Cross and the Christian, Crossway, 2021.

Philips M: The World Turned Upside Down: the global battle over God, truth and power; Encounter Books, 2011.

Plato: The Republic, Penguin Classics (Paperback ed), 2007.

Pluckrose H & Lindsay: Cynical Theories, Pitchstone, 2020.

Pollack S.D et al: Progress in understanding the emergence of human emotions; Developmental Psychology, Vol 55 no 9; 1801-1811, American Psychological Association, 2019.

Rhodes C: Woke Capitalism, How Corporate Morality is Sabotaging Democracy, Bristol University Press, 2022.

Richards B: The Psychology of Politics; Routledge, 2019.

Sachs D J: 20th Century Political Economy-A Brief History of Global Capitalism; Oxford Review of Economic Policy, Vol 15 no 4.

Sandel Michael J: The Tyranny of Merit, what's become of the common good? Penguin 2021.

Schaeffer F:  How should we then live? Crossway (50th anniversary edition), 2005.

Schiefer D, van der Noll J: The Essentials of Social Cohesion; A Literature Review; Soc. Indic. Res. (2017) 132-579-603; Science & Business Media, Springer, Dordrecht 2016.

Shorter A: Multiculturalism, Polity Press, 2022.

Stetzer ed: Christians in the Age of Outrage, Nav Press 2018.

Strachan O: Christianity & Wokeness, Salem Books, 2021.

Thiel M: The "Militant" Democracy, Principle in Modern Democracies, Routledge 2016.

Thrupp J et al: Australia Tomorrow, Connor Court 2021.

Villa, Dana R: Introduction: the Development of Arendt's Political Thought; Cambridge Companion to Hannah Arendt, 2006.

Wahl-Jorgensen K: Emotions, Media and Politics, John Wiley & Sons, 2019.

Wang W & Skovira R.J: Authenticity & Social Media, Robert Morris University, 2017.

Watkin C. Biblical Critical Theory, Zondervan Academic, 2022.

Wolf M., The Crisis of Democratic Capitalism, Penguin, 2023.

Zimmerman A & Moens G, The Unlucky Country, Locke Press 2024.

## Articles & Reports

Accelerating the Digital Future of our Australian Public Service, Digital Government Agency, Commonwealth of Australia, 2021.

An AI Action Plan for all Australians; Discussion Paper, Dept of Industry, Science & Energy Resources, Commonwealth of Australia, 2020.

Australian Cohesion Index 2023, Scanlon Foundation Research Institute, Australian University, Canberra.

Digital platforms' efforts under the Australian Code of Practice on Disinformation & Misinformation, Second Report to Government, Aust. Communications & Media Authority, July 2023.

Disrupting disadvantage and finding what works, Committee of Economic Development of Australia (CEDA), Melbourne, 2023.

Human Rights & Technology Final Report Summary; Australian Human Rights Commission, Sydney, 2021. Listen Loudly, Act Strongly, Independent Review into ABC Systems and Processes in Support of Staff who Experience Racism, 2024, https://liveproduction.wcms.abccdn.net.au/726cda3b8b2694c d1714c3c5ada5254c, accessed 03/10/2024.

Safe & Responsible AI, Australian Government Interim Response, Dept of Industry, Science & Resources, Commonwealth of Australia, 2024.

Many experts say digital disruption will hurt democracy, Pew Research Centre, Feb.21 2020.

Five-year productivity inquiry: keys to growth- Inquiry Report - Vol. 2, Report 100, Productivity Commission, Commonwealth of Australia, 2023.

2030 Digital Decade, Report on the State of the Digital Decade, European Commission, Project no 2023-4792.

Unsafe at Work, Assaults on Journalists, Media Entertainment & Arts Alliance (MEAA) Report on the State of Press Freedom in 2021, Mike Dobbie, Redfern NSW, 2021.

Other titles by this author:

*Silent, Fragile and Isolated*

www.ingramcontent.com/pod-product-compliance
Lightning Source LLC
Chambersburg PA
CBHW032056020426
42335CB00011B/372